THE Lazy Girl's GUIDE TO Life

100+ WAYS TO HACK YOUR LOOK LOVE WORK

*** BY DOING **(ALMOST)** NOTHING! ***

Jennifer Byrne

Adams Media
New York London Toronto Sydney New Delhi

Adams Media
An Imprint of Simon & Schuster, Inc.
57 Littlefield Street
Avon, Massachusetts 02322

First Adams Media hardcover edition SEPTEMBER 2017

Interior design by Michelle Roy Kelly

Manufactured in the United States of America

10 9 8 7 6 5 4 3 2 1

Library of Congress Cataloging-in-Publication Data has been applied for.

ISBN 978-1-5072-0445-0
ISBN 978-1-5072-0446-7 (ebook)

Contains material adapted from the following titles published by Adams Media, an Imprint of Simon & Schuster, Inc.: *Fake It* by Jennifer Byrne, copyright © 2012, ISBN 978-1-4405-4109-4; *Just Clean Enough* by I.B. Caruso and Jenny Schroedel, copyright © 2011, ISBN 978-1-4405-0656-7.

INTRODUCTION

An organized living space. A productive workday. Clear skin, fantastic hair, and a kickass social life.

Sounds nice, right?

Look, we all want to look like we have it together, but it's really tough to get your act in gear when you'd rather spend your time lounging around in your leggings, scrolling through social media, and eating Funfetti cupcakes—just because you can.

Enter *The Lazy Girl's Guide to Life*. Here you'll find some pretty amazing hacks that will enable you to function passably in the real world while expending as little energy and time as possible. This will free you up for what is really important, like watching a YouTube video of a turtle dressed up like a sandwich. (Which is super adorable, btw.)

Okay, but what is a lazy girl, exactly?

A lazy girl is a person who, instead of making to-do lists, makes "I can't even" lists (or better yet, no lists at all). A lazy girl is someone who would rather never find out which celebrity moms ate their own placentas than have to click through *one. more. page*. of that annoying slideshow. A lazy girl is someone who doesn't bother to edit her phone's autocorrect, and who therefore is constantly texting about "giving zero ducks." Sound familiar? (No judgment here—I'm a lazy girl too.)

So take the hacks that you'll find throughout the book and pretend you're one of those mythical people who have it all together. Fake your clean laundry, don't tell anyone you forgot to make that dinner reservation, and make it look like you're absolutely incredible at your job. Because seriously, behind every great woman there is a lazy girl, just kind of reclining in the background and constantly hitting "snooze."

PART 1

Looking Presentable

As a lazy girl you'd almost certainly prefer to spend the day on the couch binge-watching Netflix than go to some stupid bridal shower, brunch, or, you know, your job. But messy buns and leggings will only take you so far and you do occasionally have to pull it together and leave the house. And when you do, you want to look great. Fortunately, you don't have to try that hard to make yourself more-than-presentable. In this part, you'll learn how to fake clean hair, shaved legs, and flawless skin. You'll also find tips on the least-exhausting ways to look toned AF—and you don't have to set foot anywhere near a gym. So yes, you're a lazy girl, but that doesn't mean you have to look like one . . .

PROBLEM

You Need Clean Hair, but Taking a Shower Is So Much Work

Ugh, the burdensome task of washing your hair. The last time you tried to do it, it totally took all night . . . or at least it felt like it did. If only you didn't have to lather/rinse/repeat. If only you didn't have to deal with shampoo *and* conditioner. If only you could just hide in the house and forget the whole thing . . .

In any case, it's been a while since you embarked on that dreaded hair-washing chore, and it's starting to show. Your hair looks limp and stringy, and you're at the point where even a ponytail can't save you.

But don't worry—there's hope! All that oil that looks so gross right now? It's moisturizing your hair like nature's leave-in conditioner—for free. So when you wash it next, all those people who were calling you "Greased Lightning" will have to step back and bask in the splendor of your shiny, lustrous hair. In the meantime, though, here are some lazy girl, clean hair hacks that will get you looking great with minimal work . . . because we all know you're not actually going to hop in the shower, right?

Lazy Girl Hack: Use Dry Shampoo

If you didn't have the time or energy to wash your hair this morning, don't worry. You can stop the oil slick by using dry shampoo.

Dry shampoos usually come as light, quick-drying spray or powder, and you just need to apply and comb through your hair evenly. Dry shampoos absorb the oil and create the illusion of fastidious hygiene even as you ponder the idea of offering your hair as an alternate fuel source. There are a couple of things to keep in mind, though.

One is that these products often have a "matte" effect, so your hair might look a bit on the dull side. But of course, *dull* is the opposite of "glistening with oil," right? That said, if you really feel that you need shiny hair for a specific reason, you can look for an additional spray to add shine (some hair powder labels include recommendations for shine products).

You Know You're a Lazy Girl When . . .

Getting caught in a downpour with heavy winds is close enough to a "wash and blow-dry" for you.

Two is that sometimes the powder in the dry shampoo can make your hair look like it's turning gray. So absolutely brush this stuff through your hair until it's fully absorbed. But if that sounds like too much work, just spray and go. Better to look like you have a few grays than to look like you were too lazy for personal hygiene . . .

Lazy Girl Hack: Only Wash the Front of Your Head

If you have or have ever had bangs, you know that the hair that seems to get the greasiest is the hair that sits right above your eyes. If you have bangs, you know it's that one horrible lock that curves greasily into your sightline. If you don't, it's pretty much all the hair that touches your face.

You Know You're a Lazy Girl When . . .

Just wearing your hair down counts as making an effort.

The good news is that there's a quick fix that will get you out of the house in no time. Just pull the rest of your hair back, do a quick wash of only your bangs or the hair by your face, then hit that hair with your blow-dryer. Style as usual and you're out the door with a seemingly clean head of hair—and no one will know the difference. Good job, lazy girl!

Lazy Girl Hack: Just Cover It Up

The most obvious solution for dirty hair is to simply slap a lid on that stuff: a hat, a bandanna, a tiara, whatever. It depends on the situation, obviously, and if you're attending a weekend sporting event outside or it's winter, you've hit the lottery. You can put on a winter hat and be done with it. If it's summer and you're headed to an outdoor date, put on a pretty bandanna or headband. If it's Monday and you have to give a presentation to your bosses, a braid, an updo, or even parting your hair in a slightly different place can also make your hair look less greasetastic. And if you're going somewhere fancy schmancy, razzle-dazzle the crowd and rock the hell out of that tiara. Everyone will be so focused on what you have on your head that they won't pay any attention to what's actually going on with your hair. Plus, you get to wear a tiara, so it's really a win-win.

PROBLEM

You Want Short Hair, but Commitment Sucks

If you have long hair and dream of the day when you can get up in the morning and not have to worry about styling, blow-drying, and all that other stuff that takes a ton of time, you're not alone. Getting a short cut seems like it would solve the problem, right? It's low-maintenance. You can just comb it and go. It's the perfect solution! But making a formal commitment to short hair just seems so scary . . .

If this sounds familiar, don't worry! You can have short hair and still rock a ponytail. You can have short hair without having to spend a year growing your hair out again. You can have short hair without the sick feeling of buyer's remorse.

Well . . . actually you can't. But what you can do is fake a short cut—lazy girl style!

Lazy Girl Hack: Be a Pinup Girl

You're not the only cut-o-phobe out there—you share your inability to muster up the fortitude to commit with lots of celebrities, models, and fashion designers. Just when you think your favorite celeb has chopped off her locks, you discover that it was an ingenious illusion created by those magician hairstylists. Then you learn that it's as simple as a few bobby pins, an elastic band, and opposable thumbs. Emily Hebert at

Elle.com says you can create a faux "asymmetrical pixie" by creating a deep side part, pulling hair back, and fastening it in the back, allowing a few strands to show for a casually "mussed" look.

You've also probably heard of the faux bob. Celebrities like Zendaya, Emma Watson, and Zooey Deschanel have all been seen sporting the scissorless bob around Hollywood. To get this look just pull your hair into a low, loose ponytail, secure it with a band that matches your hair color, and tuck and pin it in place with (many) bobby pins. This style works best as a tousled/casual look with wavy hair since "day-old," unwashed hair is more moldable. This is an awesome hack technique for those of you who eschew shampoo, so check it out!

Lazy Girl Hack: Wig Out

The most straightforward way to get a short "do" while still maintaining your policy of "don't" is to get yourself a wig. Don't worry: while you might not have a friendly neighborhood wig shop right up the street, you have a phone that you're always on that connects you to the world wide web. Once there, the world of the short-haired is your oyster. Some websites even sell custom celebrity-style wigs, so you can basically "scalp" the hairstyles of Katy Perry, Millie Bobby Brown, Miley Cyrus, and more (no celebrities were harmed in the making of these wigs). You can get wigs that are made of synthetic materials or you can go big and buy ones made from real hair. These real-hair wigs can get fairly pricey, though, so weigh your options. You could theoretically get a used human-hair wig at a thrift store, but here I have to ask you: Has it really come down to double-recycled human hair? Maybe a call to your local stylist isn't the worst idea in the world . . .

PROBLEM

You Want Long Hair, but Growing It Out Takes Too Long

So now that you know how to half-ass short hair (or maybe you actually went ahead and hacked it off and are now regretting it), you've been thinking about how great and easy long hair would be. Especially during the summer.

Ah, summer! It's a wonderful, easy-breezy, opened-toed-shoes-and-bare-legs-under-a-skirt time of year. It's the one time when fashion is as laid-back and as comfortable as it's going to get. Still, though, that illusion of comfortable casualness requires rigorous work, maintenance, and the discipline of a Navy SEAL. This is especially true if you're looking to get the long, lusciously tousled hair that is best suited to blowing in the breeze as you walk in slow motion down the beach or ride in a convertible. You would never forget that, would you? Surely, you've been growing your "beach hair" all winter. Right?

Yeah, okay. Growing out your hair is Just. So. Painful. Especially if you have bangs, or short hair, or hair that looks like a rat's nest once it grows past your shoulders. You wouldn't think that *not* doing something would be this terrible (and this time-consuming), but it is. The good thing is that you can totally fake that long-haired look and it doesn't even take that much work.

Lazy Girl Hack: Clip It

Lucky for you, faking longer hair has never been easier. Once upon a time, people had to resort to Elvira wigs or those Rasta hats with the fake dreadlocks. Now, you can easily get clip-on hair extensions. In some states, these can be found right in local drugstores, or online for the truly lazy girl. You can also check beauty supply stores. Some of these are decent quality and can add length or volume. Jessica Simpson currently sells a line of clip-on hair extensions, which, if all goes well for her, will extend her fifteen minutes of fame as well as your hair. These products take about five minutes to clip on and can be easily removed when you're done gallivanting at the beach and are ready to slip back into your pajama pants.

Lazy Girl Hack: Just Spring for the Hair Extension Already

Professional hair extensions are also much easier—and much higher quality—than they used to be. They are still a bit of a commitment, though, and are more time-consuming and costly than the clip-ons. That said, when you're tossing that windswept hair around on the beach in front of admiring eyes, it's less likely to fall off your head and blow into the lifeguard's face if it's a professional job. These extensions are often either sewn or glued onto your natural hair and "grow out" after about four to six months.

PROBLEM

You Want Beach Hair, but Hate Going to the Beach

If you're the type of person who dreads heading to the beach, you have good reason. Going to the beach is a flippin' project. First you have to shop for a bathing suit, which is the worst! Then you have to get up early and pack a ton of stuff to bring with you: food, drinks, sunscreen, a hat, a towel, a beach chair, something to read . . . Then you have to drive to the beach and spend forever looking for parking, only to find that you have to park five miles away and pay a ton of money for it. Then you have to lug all that stuff that you packed down to the beach (in one trip, of course), burn your feet on the sand, find a place to sit, set up shop . . . the list goes on and on.

But even though you don't really want to put in the effort to actually *go* to the beach, you still want your hair to look like you did. And the good thing is that now, it can.

Lazy Girl Hack: Get Some Highlights

The first step to getting that sought-after beach look is to get some sun-kissed color. But just take a minute to think first—do you want to artificially damage your hair even more than you would with the sun? Of course not! There's nothing worse than a bad, streaky bleach job under garish fluorescent lights. So proceed wisely. According to celebrity colorist Eva Scrivo at Elle.com, you might want to avoid the traditional "foil" highlights, for two reasons: One, foil highlighting works with four- to five-inch sections of hair at a time, which often results in overhighlighting. Two, the foils are a conductor of heat, which is damaging and can cause a "brassy" color. Instead, Scrivo recommends the balayage method of coloring, which involves highlighting as much or as little hair as you want, allowing for a more natural result. Remember, if you don't leave some dark in, there's nothing to show the highlights against. If you highlight everything, you're not really highlighting anything. Got it?

You Know You're a Lazy Girl When . . .
You go out of your way to take the ramp down to the beach because you're too lazy to use the stairs.

Lazy Girl Hack: Wave Hello

An important component of beach hair is a gorgeous wave. You know how amazing your hair looks when it dries after you swim in the ocean? According to www.collegefashion.net, most of us have a certain amount of natural wave to our hair, and you can bring out your natural beach hair by spraying your hair with salt. Yes, salt, which makes you bloated when you eat it and causes slugs to melt on the sidewalk, is actually a good idea for your summer hair. Specifically, products called "salt sprays" are designed to create those "beachy" waves. Salt sprays can be drying, though, so it's best not to use them every day unless your goal is to look authentically beach-damaged.

For extra wave, you can use a large-barreled curling iron, or braid your hair at night while it's still damp and then sleep on it. This seems like more work than just spraying your hair with salt water, but either way, even if the only surfing you do is at your laptop, you're still going to have the best beach hair in town!

PROBLEM

You Want Bangs, but Aren't Sure If You Can Pull Them Off

You and bangs—throughout your life, it's been a turbulent, love-hate relationship. The first time you and bangs met, it was the day before second-grade school pictures, when your BFF Kimmy gave you a "bowl cut" in her basement. You didn't even have to fake being sick on picture day—you were vomiting out of genuine disgust and horror.

This set the course for the rest of your life. Even after those bangs grew out, bangs have always prompted a complex mix of longing, hesitation, and outright fear in you. "Should I, or shouldn't I?" is the "big bang" question in your life, and it tends to crop up every few years. Your dream is that your face will be adorably and stylishly transformed. Your nightmare is that you just aren't the type of person who can handle a bang.

And, seriously, bangs are so much work! Sometimes they're more cow(lick) than wow and keeping them in line involves hair products, straighteners, and blow-dryers and you spend all your time constantly trying to figure out if you have the right kind of round brush . . . It's pretty intense. But relax! You don't have to commit to bangs until you are good and ready. And that time may be never, but you can still try out this lazy girl trick to faking high-maintenance bangs and no one will be the wiser.

Lazy Girl Hack: Make Your Own

Honestly, faking bangs is pretty easy. All you really need is a brush, a headband, and a few bobby pins. Start by making a high, tight ponytail on the top of your head, pretty much right where your messy bun sits when you're not trying to impress anyone. Then, take the front part of the ponytail and flop the end of the hair down over your forehead so it looks like bangs. Lift the hair so your "bangs" are the desired length, and then pin down your fake bangs with bobby pins placed close to the base of the ponytail. Then you can use either a headband or a bandanna to cover the extra hair pinned up on the top of your head or you can take some hair from the back of the ponytail, divide it in two, and wrap it around the ponytail to create a bun. No one will know the difference and this look is super easy to achieve. It's a total win-win!

Lazy Girl Hack: Pin Them In

If you don't feel skilled enough to manipulate your own hair into bangs, don't worry. You can always buy clip-in bangs. These can be found online, in beauty supply stores, or from stores like Urban Outfitters, and have been sported by celebs like Chrissy Teigen, Gigi Hadid, Karlie Kloss, and sundry members of the Jenner/Kardashian clan. When using the clip-ins, make sure to choose a color that's as close to your hair color as possible (you want to stand out because you have awesome hair, not because you're blatantly faking) and choose a cut that works for your face. For example, if you have a narrow face, clip in some blunt bangs. If your face is round, choose bangs that are a little longer at the sides to frame your face. Then, once you clip in the bangs, put some of your actual hair over them so no one can see the transition, and style as usual.

And, voila! You have bangs that will see you through the night, but are made with someone else's effort. Lazy girls rejoice!

PROBLEM

You Waxed Your Own Eyebrows and Totally Screwed Up

Okay, let's be honest. Finding the time to head to the hair salon just to have someone pour hot wax on your face and rip part of your eyebrows off isn't anyone's idea of a good time. So you thought you'd order one of those kits online and try it yourself. After all, how hard could it be?

It's hard! Really hard—and really painful! The people who do this at the salon are trained professionals who do this for a living. Next time, you're going to have to suck it up and let them do their jobs, but fortunately, for now, you can still get out of the house without anyone knowing what you've done to yourself. How? Read on . . .

Lazy Girl Hack: Pencil It In

For short-term goals, such as not looking like a permanently shocked crazy woman tonight, you need to pick up your pencil and get to work like you're taking the SATs. If you have pale eyebrows, says Jenny Bailly on www.oprah.com, you should choose a color that is two shades darker than your natural color, and if your brows are dark, you should choose a color that is two shades lighter. Use the pencil to gently trace along the brows' upper edges, then fill in the inner corners and ends with light strokes. Don't press down too hard, and don't ever use black pencil! No one looks sane with overdone, dramatic brows. Bailly also recommends penciling in your eyebrows before you apply your eye makeup. Maybe you can deal with your eyebrows at home after all!

PROBLEM

Your Eyes Are Puffy . . . and People Are Starting to Ask Questions

Maybe you've been out all night painting the town red, or maybe you've been in all night repainting the walls burnt umber (*hello*, that house isn't going to remodel itself!). Perhaps you and your amazing new soul mate couldn't bear to fall asleep for even a second (you'd miss each other!). Maybe you're a wild bohemian who lives a restless lifestyle. Or maybe, and perhaps most likely, you stayed up all night binge-watching new releases on Netflix and totally forgot that you have to adult today.

Whatever the reason (it's totally Netflix, right?), it's been a few days since you've slept, and your eyes are giving you away. They're bloodshot, puffy, and about half their usual size and radiance. If they are, in fact, a window to your soul, your soul is looking a little fried. Time for a hack worthy of a lazy girl!

Lazy Girl Hack: De-Puff

The first thing your eyes need is for you to deflate the puffy, parade-float lids that are stealing the show from your actual eyeballs. And part of the way to do this is cold and caffeine. And, no,

I'm not talking about an iced mochaccino, although, what the hell, go ahead and have one of those too.

Look for an eyelid gel or serum that contains caffeine and peptides, which act to boost collagen while reducing puff. To really maximize that effect, pop these products in the fridge first. You'll find the coolness soothing, and it will also reduce the swelling.

Lazy Girl Hack: Create an Illusion

Makeup is the single most important tool at your disposal for faking big, bright eyes after serious sleep loss. Fortunately, according to YouTube makeup guru Michelle Phan, there are specific colors and applications that can brighten and open up tired, droopy eyes. Phan suggests starting by lining your lower lids with white eyeliner. Next, apply a light-colored eye shadow to your upper lids, and use a silver eye shadow on your upper brow line and near your tear ducts (if you've been crying, wait until you're finished first). If you need to pencil or shade in your eyebrows, do that. Lastly, curl your eyelashes with one of those little torture-device-looking things, and then apply mascara, holding a business card behind your upper lashes while applying, so you can get each lash. Hopefully, if you manage to create the illusion of alert normalcy, this won't be the last time you use your business cards today!

PROBLEM

You Want Great Skin, but Yours Is a Hot Mess

So, one morning, you woke up and noticed your face looks like a Domino's five-topping flaky crust special. You have blackheads, whiteheads, and possibly even redheads (they're so feisty and tempestuous!), oil slicks next to frown lines, and pores so huge you're thinking you might be able to rent them out as apartments (no smoking, pets negotiable). And of course this is the day of your big job interview, your passport photo appointment, and—worst of all—your first date with that promising guy you met at your cousin's wedding.

It looks like all those nights of not bothering to wash your face before you went to bed have taken their toll, but all is not lost. You can fix this. If makeup artists can manage to make Madonna not look like an ancient Komodo dragon, there's absolutely hope for you.

Note: These hacks work best if you do all of them consecutively, but they each work on their own as well . . . you know, in case getting through all three just seems like overdoing it.

Lazy Girl Hack: Fake, but Don't Cake

An important step to faking perfect skin is to apply a primer or a moisturizer. If your skin is not properly moisturized, the rest of your makeup is more likely to cake awkwardly around lines and other flaws, making them stand out even more. And while cake is pretty freaking amazing, there's a time and a place for everything. So put on primer or moisturizer, wait a few seconds, and then apply your concealer. Goodbye lines, hello smooth skin!

You Know You're a Lazy Girl When . . .
You never bothered to wash the boxed hair color off your skin, and now part of your actual face is dyed L'Oréal #R57, Intense Medium Auburn.

Lazy Girl Hack: Wield Your Concealer Wisely

Concealer is definitely your friend, but think of it as being like that friend who drinks one too many rum-and-Cokes and then starts crying about her unrequited crush and singing Michael Bublé songs before passing out. Less is more. It's best to choose a shade that's one or two shades lighter than your foundation, which should match your skin exactly.

Dab the concealer under your eyes, around your nose, and on any other spots that are red or discolored. Then pat it gently, blending it in so that the discolored areas look brighter. Although this brightening is awesome and you might be tempted to add a ton more, please resist. Try to respect the fact that many people have deep-seated fears of mimes and clowns.

Lazy Girl Hack: Find Your Foundation

It's time to talk foundation. The good thing is that you probably don't need to apply foundation to your entire face, just the areas that need coverage. Your foundation shade should match your natural skin tone as closely as possible, so you don't get those telltale lines of demarcation around your jawline.

The foundation you use should be tailored to whether you have dry skin or oily skin. For those of us who suffer from the multiple personality disorder of skin, politely known as "combination skin," the choice can be more confusing. For us, it is difficult to tell from day to day—even moment to moment—whether our skin belongs at the prom or the nursing home. Of course, you can try one of those "smart" foundations specifically made for combination skin (if you're wondering how they know where to moisturize and where to de-oil, it's best not to think too hard about it). If this doesn't work, you can keep two separate foundations for either situation, and decide each day if your skin is oilier or drier.

Finally, brush on a light dusting of powder, like fairy dust, and check out the amazing magic you've conjured up. Wow! You look gorgeous, and your skin doesn't resemble pizza or cake. I'd say that entitles you to a slice of each!

PROBLEM

You Need a Manicure, but Who Has the Time?

Lately you've been such a busy multitasker that you really could use several extra pairs of hands, like that Hindu goddess, what's-her-name. Of course, if you did have several extra pairs of hands, it would only highlight how badly in need of a manicure all of those hands are.

Here you thought you were on top of your beauty priorities—or were at least making it look like you are—but your hands are flaking off winter skin and have cuticles gone wild, chipped polish from two months ago, and a "manicure" administered nervously by your own teeth. Your hands have sold you right down the river.

You really can't blame yourself, though. It's tough to find the time to sit down and let yourself be pampered. Especially when you know you're just going to pick at your cuticles when you're lazily checking social media later on that night. But it looks like that CVS hand cream isn't cutting it anymore and it's time to man(icure) up and at least pretend to care about your hands.

Lazy Girl Hack: Go for a Quick Fix

If you're just about to leave the house and you realize your hands make Edward Scissorhands's hands look neat and well maintained, you need a quick fix. Fortunately, you can achieve a beautifully manicured look in about five minutes with really minimal effort. First, apply cuticle oil (or baby oil) to the base of your nails, and use a cuticle stick (or your other nails because, let's be honest, who has a cuticle stick?) to gently push your cuticles back. This creates a neat appearance and makes your nails look a little bit longer. Then buff your nails with a nail buffer, passing it over each nail in only one direction until the nail is smooth. You can then create the shape of your nails with an emery board, again filing in only one direction. Apply some clear nail polish (so you don't have to worry about painting more than your nails), let it dry, then finish up by using some hand cream, and out the door you go with no one the wiser.

Lazy Girl Hack: Try Dry

There are few things more annoying to a lazy girl than waiting for nail polish to dry. You can't touch anything, you can't pick anything up, and you're stuck fanning yourself flamboyantly like a character in *Steel Magnolias*. You can't check your phone, you can't text your friends, you can't change the channel. It's pretty much torture.

If you'd prefer a freshly applied polish job without having to wait around, there's a faster way: dry nail appliqués. These are dry strips of nail polish that are flexible and can be molded to your nails to create a faux manicure look. You can smooth them out and use a nail file to remove any extra material. Dry polish lasts about two weeks, and the polish can be removed just like any other polish—with nail polish remover or by casually picking it off as you watch TV. No fanning, no incapacitating wait. How handy!

PROBLEM

You Haven't Shaved Your Legs, but Want to Rock a Dress

You've been invited to a party in March, that schizophrenic month that can't quite seem to decide whether it wants to be winter or spring. In your world, though, it's still winter. Your legs, especially, have not gotten the memo that spring is approaching. In fact, looking at them, you might think it's the dead of winter in the Antarctic ice sheet.

Of course, the day of the party dawns bright, sunny, and with temperatures expected in the high 70s. You have an adorable sundress that would be perfect for this event, if only your legs weren't insulated with several coats of winter fur. They say March comes in like a lion and goes out like a lamb—I'd say you're going out like a lamb, my friend. A very woolly, woolly lamb.

Okay, you're a lazy shaver. No surprise there. Show me a woman who keeps her legs shiny and smooth all winter long, and I'll show you an overachiever. That said, you need to have a contingency plan in place for unseasonably warm days . . . unless you want to claim you're wearing leg warmers.

Lazy Girl Hack: Hose It Down

You remember nude pantyhose, right? Those weird things that hatched like aliens out of silver eggs in the seventies and eighties, and made your mom's legs look unnervingly tan and shiny? Those things that bank robbers wore to make their faces all squishy and indistinguishable? "But those are way out of style," you might say. Well, you're wrong.

You Know You're a Lazy Girl When . . .

You wear pants on a 90-degree day simply because you didn't feel like shaving your legs.

Pantyhose have seen a surprising comeback, thanks to the Duchess of Cambridge, Catherine Middleton. Kate has been seen flashing shiny nylon gams all over Buckingham Palace, causing people to wonder if sheer hose are actually back. It's been hinted that she's wearing the nudes not as a fashion statement, but merely in compliance with royal family prudery, which insists that women cloak all shameful below-the-waist appendages. The point is, if you have just a *slight* shadow of stubble, nude hose could provide coverage while still maintaining the look of "bare" legs. If nothing else, the fact that you're actually wearing nude hose will take attention away from the fact that you have hairy legs. And then you can go rob a bank!

Lazy Girl Hack: Just Rip It Out

If pantyhose aren't going to cut it, never fear, you have many options of the slightly-more-uncomfortable-but-longer-lasting variety. There are epilators, which consist of a million little electric springs or tweezers that yank your hairs out from the roots. There's waxing, which involves slathering wax on your hairy legs and wrenching them out at the count of three. There's also electrolysis and laser, which literally murder your hair.

You Know You're a Lazy Girl When . . .
You'd rather bleed out from your sloppy-ass shaving job than have to read the fifteen-step instructions for that home waxing kit.

In addition, there are many products sold for home use that claim to provide "painless" and "permanent" hair removal. They can be found everywhere from Sephora to As Seen On TV websites. Keep in mind, though, that electrolysis is currently the only method the FDA calls permanent. This is because it kills your hair follicles with a jolt of electricity for the crime of producing dark, manly hairs. Finally, justice is done!

That said, you could always just make sure you always have a bottle of Nair on hand and burn the hair right off your legs. It's not painless, but it sure is quick and easy.

PROBLEM

You Want Rock-Hard Abs, but Don't Want to Go to the Gym

It's summer again already—can you even believe it? Who saw that coming?

Actually, maybe it shouldn't be *that* hard to believe, after all these years. I mean, given the fact that you've had decades of summers predictably following springs and preceding falls *every single time*, you'd think you might have caught on by now. But no, like most of us, you're caught totally off-guard by it suddenly going from maximum-clothing-protected season to utter-exposure-and-humiliation season. You have not spent the winter working out. You are the color of Cream of Wheat, your muscle tone is a self-esteem booster for jellyfish, and your muffin top has become an entire bakery. You're going to the beach tomorrow, don't own a one-piece suit, and don't want to spend the day hot and bothered covered up. Ugh. You know there's no time for a crash diet, and realistically speaking, there's probably not enough time to start loving yourself and your womanly curves, either. No, in this kind of pinch, there's nothing to be done but fake a six-pack.

You Know You're a Lazy Girl When . . .

You say F it and throw on a fake abs T-shirt. This way people will focus on how funny you are, not that you couldn't get your unmotivated behind to the gym.

Lazy Girl Hack: Try Shock Treatment

This option is the ultimate lazy girl's way to get a six-pack! Have you seen those electric shock ab belts that are now on the market? These items hark back to old-school vibrating belts, and also to early twentieth-century torture devices. The concept is that by electrically shocking your ab muscles, the muscles will be forced to "work out" by flexing involuntarily. Just flip the switch that conducts the current, and . . . it lives! It tones! It gives you great abs and all you have to do is lie down on the couch! You can even get ones that you can control from your smartphone!

If shocking the crapola out of yourself so you don't have to do sit-ups doesn't sound like it's for you, there are also belts that heat up or help you retain the heat from the area around your waist. This is supposed to both get rid of the bloating you can get from excess water in your belly and remove any toxins that may have built up in your system. Seems like all you have to do is suck up any discomfort and you won't have to suck it in at the beach.

Lazy Girl Hack: Give Yourself an Ab Makeover

Probably the best approach to producing faux six-pack abs is also the easiest—just give your stomach a makeover. This sounds crazy, but you can actually just use makeup to produce subtle, humiliation-sparing abs for that first terrifying beach venture.

Start with a color of foundation that is just slightly darker than your regular skin color. Blend it with sunscreen and rub it in evenly. Then take some mineral powder that's a shade darker than the foundation, and use it to shade in some sculpted areas where a six-pack would be. Don't overdo it, or people might wonder if you've been stabbed. Finally, dust over the whole area with some bronzy powder to produce a shimmery glow.

This approach is mostly intended to jump-start your confidence for beach season since it's going to wash off pretty quickly, but you can always run to the bathhouse when you get out of the water to reapply. But after a day in the sun, you might have some natural color to improve the so-called "situation." Or even better, maybe you just won't care because you're having such a great time.

PROBLEM

You Want Killer Legs, but Hate Leg Day

It's miniskirt season, and you have a pair of legs that won't quit. You kind of wish they would quit, though, because you've been seriously thinking of firing them. As legs go, they really don't follow even your most basic instructions, such as "Be thin, appear several inches longer than you are, stop rubbing up against each other—that's so disgusting." You've spoken to the HR department in your head about how best to let these legs go, but you've been advised that because of the whole standing-up-and-helping-you-walk thing, you really do need to keep them on. Sigh. All you can do is suck it up and hope they will give their two weeks' notice.

Sadly, not all of us are naturally blessed with the long, lean legs that miniskirts were created to show off, and since you're constantly skipping leg day at the gym to hang out at home, your chances of getting great legs are looking slim to none.

But while it's true that legs can be a very stubborn body part even if you are working out, there are plenty of quick tricks you can use to put on that miniskirt and take the world by storm (not a thunder thigh storm, either!).

Lazy Girl Hack: Let the Lymph Flow

You may have already tried to get slimmer legs by restricting calories, cutting carbs, eating nothing but cabbage soup, and whatever other deprivation craze came to your attention. (Or maybe you just sat back and thought about how good being able to do all those things would be.) And while some of these diets may have helped you lose overall weight, they've never really helped take the thunder out of your thighs. According to French beauty publicist Marie-Laure Fournier, the best way to remove all that cellulite that's stuck in your thighs is to go for something called lymphatic drainage. This is basically a kick-ass massage that jump-starts the lymphatic system. How can that help, you ask? Well, the lymphatic system helps flush toxins from your body, and when the lymph is slow or ineffective, it can retain toxins and cause bulkier legs. Fournier says, "Lymphatic drainage is the best beauty regime you can do without exercise. No matter what, you do need to do it, for everything. If you have heavy legs or blood-circulation problems, you need to do it." Nice. *Go lie down and get a massage right now so that your legs will be thinner.* That is the kind of command a lazy girl likes to obey.

Lazy Girl Hack: Create a Media Blitz

One way to get killer legs without moving from your couch is to simply redefine the public perception of what killer legs are. I mean, who would have seen the "big butt" trend coming? If big butts got to be so popular that women were buying padded panties, who's to say big thighs won't have their day in the sun? The fastest way to popularize chunky legs is to spread a rumor that some celebrity either has or wants them. Start a blog that speculates, "Are so-and-so's huge thighs real, or is she wearing silicone fakes?" Discuss how all the celebs are getting thigh fat injections and cankle implants. Plant the seed, sit back, and watch it grow. Note: This could possibly take a long time, maybe even your whole lifetime. But your grandkids—if you insist on continuing your thigh genetics—will get to walk around in the teeniest of skirts with pride. It's a beautiful legacy (pun intended).

PROBLEM

You Want a Tattoo, but Don't Want the Pain

Lately, it seems you've become obsessed with the idea of getting a tattoo. Maybe it's the lure of gorgeous celebrities with cool ink, or maybe you've met someone amazing whose name you're just dying to have emblazoned on your body for all time, or maybe you just really love your mom. Whatever your reasons, you've been looking up Chinese characters online, asking tattooed friends to rate the pain from one to ten, and leafing through *The Girl with the Dragon Tattoo* in search of illustrations (there are none—what a ripoff *that* book is).

So what's stopping you? Well, tattoos are just so *permanent*, or at least semipermanent. How can you be sure you're still going to love this guy Chip when you're eighty years old? (If you get his name on your hip, though, you can pull a Johnny Depp and edit your tattoo to say "hip." You'll look like a textbook anatomy chart, which might help the surgeon who eventually does your hip replacement.) How can you be sure your mom isn't going to seriously annoy you sometime soon? And how can you guarantee that the Chinese character really does translate to "New Beginnings" and not "Kick me, I'm a total sucker!"?

Lazy Girl Hack: Get a Hypothetical Tattoo

The first step to faking a tattoo is getting a hypothetical one first, using your imagination. This hypothetical tattoo will serve the purpose of showing you the potential roadblocks and future problems you might have. You can then adjust your life accordingly. For example, if you're dating a guy named David, your only post-breakup editing option would be to change it to "avid." If you do this, you'll have to add something like "birdwatcher," or "doll collector," just so it makes sense, and then take up that hobby. Likewise, if your true love is named "Jonathan" and you're not 100 percent sure of him, you should acquire a good friend named Nathan who is secretly in love with you. Nathan will be an excellent backup in case you catch Jonathan making out with your best friend in the Olive Garden bathroom during your birthday dinner. Not that such a thing has ever happened to anyone I know.

Lazy Girl Hack: Get a Cereal Box Tattoo

Remember when you were a kid and would get those temporary tattoos out of a cereal box or a gumball machine? True, they might have been of the Care Bears or Rainbow Brite or the Power Rangers, but so what? You just put the tattoo on your skin, pressed down with a wet sponge, and voilà! You had a tattoo. These are easy, totally commitment-free alternatives to getting real ink. In fact, they're so commitment-free that if you accidentally rub up against something, or look at them too hard, they might peel right off. What did you expect from a Lucky Charms prize? Seriously, though, classy temporary tattoo designers like Paperself and Marbella Paris now offer their grown-up version of these childhood favorites. Too bad they don't make a cereal too!

Lazy Girl Hack: Make Your Own

If you're more of a DIY type, you can actually create your own temporary tattoo using permanent markers. According to a tutorial from artist Makeupholicliz, you can create a tattoo using a picture of your desired image, a tattoo pencil (sold at craft stores), tracing paper, scissors, alcohol-based deodorant, fine-point permanent markers, 99 percent alcohol, and Q-tips. Your first step is to use your tattoo pencil to trace the design onto the tracing paper. Once you've traced the design, carefully cut it out. Next, apply the deodorant onto your skin where you want the tattoo to be. Apply the cutout pencil-side down onto your skin and press down. Peel the paper away carefully.

Next is the fun part—break out the markers! Using a black marker, carefully trace over the outline you did in pencil. Then use your colors to slightly shade—but not fully color in—the inside of your tattoo. Next, put some of the 99 percent alcohol on a Q-tip, and dab the colored parts to blend.

If this seems like too much work, just grab a permanent marker and color on yourself while you watch TV. Either way, your ink is beautiful today, but will be long gone when you're eighty!

PROBLEM

You've Gained Some Weight, but Don't Want Photo Evidence

Imagine this scenario: You attend a friend's or family member's wedding, and you have an awesome time. You wear "That Dress"—the one that never fails you, the one that makes you feel like a movie star. Your hair is perfect, you radiate confidence, and you charm and dazzle strangers and old acquaintances alike. What a night.

A week later, one of the bridesmaids graciously posts pictures of the wedding on Facebook. They're fine, except you have one question: "Who is the bloated, multi-chinned toad that's wearing my dress?"

For those of us who aren't particularly photogenic, photos can really ruin a good time after the fact. It's like being Cinderella at the ball, and then at midnight having a horrible iPhone photo taken that transforms your head into a giant, misshapen pumpkin.

If this has happened to you, know that you're not alone. Photos capture just a millisecond in time, and if your mouth is twisted the wrong way, your chin clones itself, or your arms are squished unflatteringly at your sides, that millisecond could produce years of embarrassment.

But because you don't want to be Cinderella forever, let's discuss fakes for your next photo op.

Lazy Girl Hack: Spread Your Wings

It is possible that on this occasion you are wearing a short-sleeved or sleeveless dress. If so, make a point to hold your arms slightly away from your body to avoid what I will delicately call "arm mash." The principle is that sometimes, when you hold your arms too close to your sides, the upper arms flatten and spread against the sides, leading your flesh to look like dough that's imploded in the oven. It's very similar to the "thigh mash" that occurs when you sit down. For that reason, you might want to avoid sitting down, too, if possible. Basically, you should focus on keeping all four limbs from pressing against anything at all, even if you're posing for a picture with Brad Pitt. Sure, he's hot, but when it comes to photos, he's just a surface that will mash your fat.

Lazy Girl Hack: Strike the Pose

When you were a kid, all you knew about posing for a picture was that it was fun to make rabbit ears behind your sister's head. Today, you still make rabbit ears, just because they're the only part of you that looks thin in a photograph. (Wow, what a svelte rabbit! How *do* you do it?)

But here's the good news: You don't need to resort to weird rodent impressions to look thin anymore! There is a secret pose that women in the know have been using for years to slim their photo images. All you have to do is turn your lower body at a three-quarter angle and put one hand on your hip. It might seem like a ridiculously sassy way to stand, but just imagine you are getting ready for a gunfight at high noon. Supposedly this pose really works, so maybe after you see its results once, you won't feel like a fool doing it the next time.

Lazy Girl Hack: Keep Your Chin Up

Quite possibly the fastest way to look heavier than you are in a picture is to accidentally create the photo double chin. This instantly adds both age and weight, and causes the party host to wonder where the extra balloon came from. Don't worry! Simply stand up straight, pull your shoulders back, and stick your chin out about an inch. This won't feel even remotely natural, but do it anyway. Who needs "natural" when you know how to lazy-girl your way through a photo session?

You Know You're a Lazy Girl When . . .

You reached your step count on that Fitbit your mom gave you by moving your arm back and forth while fully seated.

PROBLEM

You Just Went on a Tropical Vacation, but Are Still Pale AF

You went on that weeklong cruise to truly unplug, relax, and get in touch with a calmer, more centered, more in-the-moment you. Well, that, and to make all your friends weep with sickening, office-bound envy over your sun-kissed skin.

The problem? When it wasn't raining torrentially, you were stuck inside your cabin praying for the end to all tidal motion. And when you were able to go outside, you remembered that you're too afraid of skin cancer to wear anything less than sunscreen with an SPF of 55. So, not only are you not gorgeously tan upon arriving home, you're somehow paler than you were when you left. What do you do now?

Lazy Girl Hack: Go on a Photoshopping Spree

If it's bragging rights you're after, all you really need is a computer and some basic Photoshop skills to edit your tan after the fact. Just google "Photoshop tan," and you'll find various tutorials on how to transform your nauseous green memories into gorgeous, sun-kissed do-overs. You can proudly post these pictures on every social media site you can think of and everyone you know will coo the expected "You're *so* lucky!" and "You look *awesome*!" comments you were angling for. The catch? You're going to have to avoid these people for a while. Actually, this isn't that bad because who the hell wants to get out there and socialize anyway? You *just* got back from a vacation where you had to talk to people every day. And your absence will only add to your exotic mystique. You'll be like everyone's elusive, golden-skinned friend—a tan unicorn.

Lazy Girl Hack: Slather Yourself in Lotions and Potions

Of course, you may decide that you actually want (or need, more likely) to interact with some human beings during the time you're faking this tan. One alternative is to use a sunless tanning lotion or gel. The good news is that you *can* do this without ending up more streaked with rust than a janitorially neglected rest stop urinal.

A trick to achieving the perfect sunless tan is to choose a level of tan that is appropriate for your natural skin color. For example, if you have naturally olive skin, you can go ahead and try products that promote a "deep" or "dark" tan. However, if you are pale as a ghost, the infusion of product on that porcelain white base will make you look like grandma's yam and marshmallow casserole.

Another modern advantage for us fakers is the invention of tinted self-tanners. These tints will enable you to detect where the product has been applied on your body, sort of like those phosphorescent lights they use on *CSI* to illuminate creepy residue on hotel beds. If you know where the stuff has been slathered, you can avoid overdoing it. *Just* like with hotel beds!

Another important tip to remember is to exfoliate before applying self-tanner. Self-tanners dye the top layer of skin, so if your top layer happens to be rough and scaly, your result will be great—if you want to look like a goldfish. If not, it's very important to take time to slough off any dead or flaky skin before you proceed.

You Know You're a Lazy Girl When . . .
You really want to get some color, but don't want to stop lying down inside to go lie down outside.

Lazy Girl Hack: Spray Away!

By now, all but the most diehard tan fans have abandoned their excessive tanning bed habits for the safer practice of spray tanning. And today many spray tan companies will come to you and tan you in the comfort of your own home, which is great! After all, if you're going to strip naked and let a stranger spray you down with a chilly liquid, you want to be comfortable.

As with the self-tanning lotion, you should prep for your spray tan by exfoliating. You should also wait eight hours after a spray tan before letting your skin get wet, and should also avoid exfoliating and shaving your legs for about a week. Hmm, so maybe you *won't* want to be seeing people after all!

PART 2

Sucking Up Social Situations

Okay, you love your friends. They're supportive and funny and awesome. But the problem with friends is that they always want you to do something with them when you'd rather be doing, you know, absolutely nothing. Right now, your social calendar is full of dreaded events like high school reunions, book club meetings, celebratory drinks, and the most dreaded event of all—family dinners. You can't get out of these things without seriously jeopardizing your friendships so you have to learn how to put on a smile and say things like "I'm so happy for you!" and "Thanks so much for inviting me!" without sounding insincere. And because you really do love your friends and typically have at least somewhat of a good time when you drag yourself out of the house, here you'll learn how to get through these social events with the least amount of effort possible.

PROBLEM

You Have Book Club, but Didn't Read the Book

It was a month ago you were "assigned" the book to read for your book club (the title involves some combination of bees, wives, and daughters), and boy, has it been a short month. The club meets tonight, and you haven't cracked that thing open at all.

Maybe it's something about the idea of being forced to read an assigned book when you're not in college anymore, or maybe you are sick of reading about bees, or maybe you've begun to notice that your book club is really just an excuse to drink copious amounts of wine and gossip about the friends who aren't invited to book club. But the fact remains, you are a book club delinquent. You hardly ever start these books, much less finish them, and so far no one is the wiser. But sooner or later, someone's going to say something about your lack of insightful comments.

You don't want to get kicked out of this club, though, so you're going to have to play along a little bit. This means doing some lazy research on *The Beekeeper's Stepdaughter's Bittersweet Honey Society*, stat.

Lazy Girl Hack: Do Some Light Reading

A great way to get an initial feel for the tone, writing, and plot of a book is to read an online synopsis, then the first couple of chapters (or just the first one . . . who are we kidding) and the last one. Book synopses are easier than ever to find—just consult Wikipedia. Read as much of it as you can manage.

Once you've read the overview of the book, take a quick spin through the first and last chapters to give you a sense of the author's style and tone. You can use this to either praise or complain about the style at your club. You can say, "Oh, I thought the author's prose style was really wordy," or "I don't think telling the story from the point of view of a pigeon was a very effective device."

You may also be lucky enough to be able to use the trump card of book critiques—hating the ending. This is very popular in book clubs. Just flip to the last chapter, and if it seems to you that maybe the ending is a bit unresolved—or worse, flat-out sad—you've just hit the book club lottery. Make sure you are the first one to say, "Am I the only one who hated the ending of this book?" and your friends will chime in with, "Oh my God! You are *so* right!" If you are the first person to mention hating the ending, you really don't have to say anything else. You've earned the right to sit back, drink your wine, and wonder who else hasn't read the book.

Lazy Girl Hack: Do Some *Super* Light Reading

If even checking out the overview and reading a couple of chapters still seems like too much work, have we got a lazy girl hack for you! Head over to the website of any bookseller and spend some time scanning the online reviews. Here you'll find a goldmine of book club discussion points ready-made into personal opinions. You may never have pictured yourself saying things like, "Once the dog died in Chapter 4, I just couldn't keep reading" or "I didn't expect this book to have so many laugh-out-loud moments, but it was insightful/enthralling/intriguing" or "I didn't want it to end. I cried when I finally closed the back cover," but you will.

And once you prove to your book club friends that you're not just there for the wine and the free food, you can finally relax. Just don't use your book as a coaster for your wineglass. That might give your true feelings away . . .

Lazy Girl Hack: Discuss the Likability of Characters

At every single book club I have ever attended, the conversation eventually works its way around to the likability of the book's characters. Even as we are discussing a literary work, we tend to fall into the habit of dissecting characters based on who we *like* or *don't like.* After all, if you're not going to gossip about your friends, you may as well gossip about the people in the book—and it's guilt-free! So it's pretty much always safe to say something like, "Am I the only one who thought Jane Eyre was a little bit of a bitch? It's like she thought she was so special and classy." Best of all, you really can't get this stuff "wrong," because it's an opinion. So you can transition smoothly between insulting your immediate supervisor at work (her skirts are made for tweens!) and insulting Hilly Holbrook from *The Help* (she *so* deserved to eat that nasty chocolate pie!). It's all just another girly bitchfest! Yay!

PROBLEM

You Run Into Someone Whose Name You Just Can't Remember

You're at a work convention, or a social event, or just walking down the street minding your own damn business, and a person you can't for the life of you remember meeting screams, "Tanya! Oh my God! It's so great to see you again, Tanya!" (By the way, your name *is* Tanya, right? If not, can I just call you that from here on out? It's just easier for me to remember.)

Anyway, this woman cannot stop repeating your name, which she has absolutely *nailed* despite the fact that you could not recall hers if a gun were pointed directly at your head. It's as if she's super proud of her memory skills, which, given the fact that you don't even remember the fact that she has ever existed, are freakishly impressive.

This is bad. You've tried little memory tricks, name recall exercises (e.g., Nancy dresses fancy), but nothing works. Unless someone has left a major and lasting impression on you, you tend to draw a massive blank. (Oh, Tanya. That's just so *you*.)

This is a common conundrum in social interactions. Particularly in the business world, where people hobnob all day long, it's hard to retain all of these names. Most people are visual learners, so it's easier to remember a face than a name. It's a shame people can't just greet each other the way dogs do, through mutual butt-sniffing. Sadly, business professionals frown on that, so what's a lazy girl to do? Well . . .

Lazy Girl Hack: Compliment Her Memory

According to Gretchen Rubin, author of *The Happiness Project*, you can defuse your poor memory by praising the other person's excellent memory. This might mean some over-the-top gushing, but it might be necessary. You can say, "Wow, I'm really impressed that you remember my name—it's been a while!" By focusing on the excellence of her memory skills, you're softening any potential insult implied by not remembering her name. You can even joke that you're going to remember her as "Person with the Awesome Memory." Actually, no, just learn her real name—you don't have the extra storage space for lengthy joke names.

Lazy Girl Hack: Introduce Him to Someone Else

Another fine trick is to introduce your new pal to a third party in your midst. Beckon over a friend or business associate, and say to the unknown person, "I'd like to introduce you to Joe Smith." At this point, custom dictates that the mystery person will state his name and shake Joe Smith's hand. If possible, you might want to have a go-to "memory buddy" who you can turn to for this one-sided introduction when you need it. In return, you can step in for her and be the third-party introduction assistant when she needs it.

If all else fails, there's nothing like searing humiliation to prod your memory the next time you see the person. When you meet him again, his face will induce a panic-filled recall of "that person who made me look like a complete idiot in front of a bunch of people." You'll never forget him again.

PROBLEM

Your Reunion Is Coming Up, but Your Life Sucks

Ah, the old high school reunion where everyone, it seems, has something to prove. And there's nothing to make you feel like you haven't reached your full potential as you walk into a room full of people who are flaunting their eight-figure jobs, their neurosurgeon husbands, or their lives in a gorgeous mansion with their 2.5 kids. (That half-kid is *so* well behaved!) Yes, you have a job that you go to every day, but you haven't found a career. You date, but you haven't found the love of your life. You have an apartment, but you have to share the bathroom with your roommate and her cat . . . Oh well, you can't do everything overnight after all. And, if there's one thing it's easy to fake, it's a fancy schmancy life at your high school reunion, so gather round and learn how.

Lazy Girl Hack: Live in the Now

In this case, you don't have to go out and buy expensive-looking jewelry or fake a boyfriend to be the belle of the ball. You just have to do a little self-faking. You need to play a little trick on your own brain in order to think about things differently.

Ditch the standard reunion measures of a "good life." Your life doesn't need to be perfect for you to appreciate how much you've changed for the better. Think of the amazing friends you have now, or the fun and challenging job, or the heartbreaks you've overcome (hint—high school is one of them!). No matter where you are on the social or economic ladder, there's no doubt you've grown. Maybe you have an amazing guy who sees you as his prom queen (even after seeing photos of your tragically bad perm and glasses), or maybe you've boldly moved to a cool city far from your hometown. No matter what else, you're a survivor. So when the cliquishness of the old high school hierarchy starts to close in on you, just click your ruby slippers and return to your *real* home—the present. (Note: Real ruby slipper clicking is not recommended. This will make you look totally insane.)

PROBLEM

Your Friend Cooks Dinner for You and It. Tastes. Awful.

A beloved friend of yours invites you to her house for dinner. It sounds great, until you get there and discover the menu.

Apparently, your once-rational friend has become somewhat of an "extreme foodie," with a leaning toward exotic (i.e., inedible) food. Tonight's menu consists of braised pork knuckles, llama bone marrow, and pickled, deep-fried octopus. The side dish is Brussels sprouts in a maple-mustard glaze.

You sit down at the table and watch your friend dish out the awfulness, all the while telling you how much you will love it. All eyes are on you—including the octopus's . . .

Lazy Girl Hack: Cough It Up

Remember the approach you used to take to gross food when you were a kid? You would put the food in your mouth, pretend to chew it, and then "politely" cover your mouth with a napkin as you started to faux cough? Try it now! Sure, it might be more complicated, given the fact that they're using fancy cloth napkins, but you can always discreetly slip the napkin into your purse or, ideally, the trash if you can manage it. This will have the time-tested effect of making food go away from your plate without it having to enter your body for anything more than a few seconds.

Lazy Girl Hack: Use the Jargon

As you subtly cough up your meal, you can really help yourself by praising the cuisine using lots of foodie adjectives. For those who consider themselves gastronomes, epicures, locavores, or gourmands, what comes out of one's mouth is almost as important as what goes in. Translation: they are wordy so-and-sos. So tell them that the llama bone marrow is "revelatory" and "piquant" and that the octopus has a "complex mouthfeel." You can talk about the "symphony of flavors" that you hear as you "tuck into" the mustardy Brussels sprouts. Say whatever, as long as it sounds really pretentious and you're not coughing up the food at the same time. Bonus points if you can work in the word "artisanal." They love that!

You Know You're a Lazy Girl When . . .

Even a lousy dinner that's made for you is better than having to get off your ass and cook for yourself.

Lazy Girl Hack: Be Sick or Full

If the previous options do not work for you and you are sure you're not going to be able to handle this meal, you need to take drastic measures to save yourself. If you are positive you can't eat any of it, you're going to have to say you're not feeling very well. You can say you went to a local bar and got a bit buzzed before dinner, and now you're feeling queasy. Or you can choose the more clichéd "I might be coming down with the flu." They may or may not believe you, but they're not going to take the chance of forcing eyeballs down your throat when it might come back up on their nice little table.

Lazy Girl Hack: Force a Bite

If you can manage to eat a little bit of one item, do it! For example, eat some complex and revelatory Brussels sprouts and say, "These are like a party in my mouth." Do what you need to do to have the table cleared and move onto dessert.

Hopefully you offered to bring dessert when you were invited for dinner. And since everyone knows you don't cook, hopefully you stopped at the fancy bakery on your way to dinner and can at least guarantee that those store-bought cookies don't contain any eyeballs. Yay!

PROBLEM

Your Friends Throw You a Surprise Party and You Hate Surprises

You've just finished doing some invariably messy and unglamorous activity—maybe it's unclogging drains at a dog salon, or Extreme Fever Hallucination Hot Yoga, or a rousing game of paintball—with your best friend, and you're wearing your please-God-don't-let-me-run-into-anyone-I-know sweatpants. So of course this is the day you will be ambushed at your home by the 1,000-kilowatt smiles of twenty of your favorite women (plus thirty other females). They are screaming, "Surprise!" as they raise their glasses of pinkish, fruit-garnished liquid in the air. You are trapped like an antelope surrounded by hungry cheetahs.

Make no mistake—surprise parties are a type of attack. Sure, they might be a *fun attack*, filled with goodwill and love, but they're attacks all the same. I mean, think about it: A large number of people have conspired to sneak up on you unawares and pounce in unison. If that happened under any other circumstances, you'd be pepper-spraying the shit out of them.

Lazy Girl Hack: Get Into the Spirit

It's perfectly fine to act thrown off—and embarrassed by your hideously inappropriate attire—for the first ten minutes or so. In fact, it's good to do this—it shows your friends that they did the job right. They got you *good*! Let them savor that depraved pleasure for a little while. After that, though, you're going to have to switch gears from "shock and horror" mode to "I'm just *delighted* to have been trapped here in these terrible sweatpants" mode. Just try to focus on your gratitude for the gesture, rather than your annoyance that you're out in public wearing your so-not-made-for-public outfit.

Lazy Girl Hack: Steal Someone's Beauty Supplies

You're in a room filled with your best friends. Hopefully at least one of them is more prepared for life than you are and carries around a tube of lipstick and a spare hair tie. Hit up that girl for everything she has and then move on to the next person who ambushed you. Maybe she has a scarf that can dress up your holey, bleach-stained T-shirt. Keep it up until you've bled your friends dry and then smile for the pictures that are sure to be taken.

Look, this isn't rocket science. Just be gracious to everyone, especially the women who worked hard to plan this for you. People will understand if you don't have much time for one-on-one conversation with each of them, but you should at least greet, chat briefly with, and thank each person at the party. Just think, some women couldn't fill a house with other people who loved them—or at least with people who didn't particularly hate them. Not if their *lives* depended on it. So feel the love!

PROBLEM

Your BFF Has a Baby and You Have No Idea What to Say

Well, the big day has come for your BFF—she's given birth to her first baby. You're over-the-moon excited for her, but you have absolutely zero experience with babies. All you know is that they cry and poop, sometimes they don't sleep, and this one in particular is probably going to keep your bestie from meeting you for happy hour.

But there's no way around it—you're going to have to figure out how to compliment this baby. Not just the baby's mere existence or the fact that he is a little miracle with ten fully functional fingers and toes, but the baby's superior adorableness. Your friend is waiting for you to say that her offspring is the most eye-pleasing creature you have ever seen, even if it's not true. And, honestly, some babies are just not cute. Especially ones that are brand-new. They tend to look like aliens or little old men and they are scary. They have no control over their arms and legs. They're tiny. And you're terrified that you might either drop this kid or hold him so tight that he's going to be damaged for life.

But no matter how weird and scary a baby is, you *cannot* tell your friend that. Ever. Women don't have babies so that they can be told terrible truths—they have babies so that they can hear lots of coos and "aws," buy little footie pajamas, hear magical music box songs, and picture frolicking lambs in their heads all day. They certainly don't do it so you can say, "That baby's so fugly, I'll bet his incubator had tinted windows."

I mean, think about it: When's the last time anyone ever said, "Here's a picture of our new baby. We welcome your honest feedback"? Right, never. That's because they don't want it. So, you're going to have to hold your tongue. When it comes to you and this baby, it is officially Opposites Day. I call this very necessary evil the "crib fib."

Lazy Girl Hack: Don't Delay!

Ideally, you should start crafting some good crib fibs as soon after birth as possible, not only because your delay would look suspicious, but also because of those freaking adorable skullcaps they slap on babies in the maternity ward. Those hats are the great equalizers of baby heads the world over. They're especially useful when the hat conceals most of the face. (Maybe someday hospitals will figure this out and start using little ski masks!) But for now, you can say something like "Aw, he looks *so* cute in his little hat!" That's not 100 percent dishonest, is it? This goes double for those anti-scratch mittens.

A great way to increase your chances of this skullcap scenario is to buy the baby a whole slew of them before he's even born, as a shower gift. Even if your friend hates them and never uses them 364 days of the year, you can almost guarantee she'll throw one on little Igor's head specifically for *your* visit. FYI, this is a secret from the Mom Bag of Tricks and Fakes—having the baby model his or her gifts specifically for the giver. So your friend will be pulling a fake on you too. Luckily, it will be a fake that happens to cover two of the baby's three eyes.

You Know You're a Lazy Girl When . . .

You love babies, but you also love handing them back to their parents when they cry/drool/poop.

Lazy Girl Hack: Use Your Friend's Good Looks to Your Advantage

If you should miss that perfect window when those caps still fit over the child's giant head, never fear (unless the little monster starts gnawing or spitting up on everything you own—then, be very afraid). Try to focus on an attractive feature your friend has, and claim that the baby also has it, such as "Look at those big blue eyes! They're just like Momma's!" Every mother wants to hear that the kid she carried around for nine months looks just like her, so if you say this, you're in the clear.

You Know You're a Lazy Girl When . . .
You are seriously jealous of how often babies get to nap.

Lazy Girl Hack: Just Be Nice

If all else fails, focus on the fact that this is your BFF's child and a sweet, innocent new life and just be nice. Say the baby is cute. Focus on how your friend is feeling. And, luckily, you won't need to fake it for too much longer, because most babies get *much* cuter within their first year, and grow out of that funky squishing of the head thing. Whew!

PROBLEM

Your Friend Breaks Up with Her Boyfriend, but You Don't Care Because You Hated Him

Did you know that at the funeral of North Korean autocrat Kim Jong Il, people who didn't cry convincingly enough were sentenced to six months in hard labor camps? Talk about being a little *too* lazy! You can bet that hundreds of people who would have much preferred to dance around singing "Ding Dong, the Dictator's Dead" were instead wringing their hands, shrieking in pseudo-agony, and chopping onions on the sly. And so it must be with you, lazy girl, as you react to the news that your friend is finally breaking up with that jerk she's been lugging around.

I mean, this guy is a grade A loser in almost every way. He's selfish, lazy, mean-spirited, and the intellectual equal of an amoeba. *And* he has a wandering eye that strays so far someone should round it up and put it in the SPCA. And yet he continues to think he is God's Gift to Women. Let's hope God had the sense to include a gift receipt with this one.

Basically, he's the Kim Jong Il of boyfriends, and he's finally been toppled. How do you pretend not to celebrate with the fervent joy of a thousand repressed societies? How do you not roll your eyes as you listen to your friend grieve her sucky relationship for the thousandth time? How do you get through your friend's breakup with this POS without having to put in more effort than he did?

Lazy Girl Hack: Buy Tubs of Ben & Jerry's and Watch *The Notebook*

Sure, you had your issues with the guy—he was a know-it-all creep who talked down to your friend (when he wasn't busy talking directly at other women's boobs)—but for whatever reason, she cared about him, and she's probably grieving the breakup. Your dance of joy would therefore be inappropriate and hurtful, but that doesn't mean you can't derive some enjoyment from the situation. So invite your friend over, pop *The Notebook* into the DVD player, and start consuming tubs of ice cream like there's no tomorrow, because let's face it, what woman doesn't love shamelessly indulging in swirls of caramel and chunks of brownies while watching Ryan Gosling carry Rachel McAdams up several flights of stairs? We women are unique in that we have our little celebratory rituals for the full range of our emotions, the bad as well as the good. In other words, even our pity parties have awesome food.

You Know You're a Lazy Girl When . . .
You eat your ice cream right out of the container so you don't have to wash any extra dishes. You know you're *really* lazy if you use a disposable spoon.

And when your friend starts bawling over how much her ex reminds her of Ryan's character (right, because you're *sure* her man also jumped up onto a moving Ferris wheel to ask her out), you can start your own waterworks by lamenting the hours you'll have to spend at the gym to burn off those five pints of Half Baked you just ate. By the end of the movie, she'll be consoling you!

Lazy Girl Hack: Don't Make Her Defend Him

A crucial mistake you want to avoid is to force your friend into the position of defending this man. No matter how much of a creep he might have been, she will be compelled to defend him if you attack him. In this way, you're essentially forcing her to recall his finer moments (yes, he took me to Hooters for Valentine's Day, but he paid, and that Lots-A-Tots appetizer was delicious!) and cite his good qualities (he always said he thinks girls with a little extra weight are beautiful!). The next thing you know, she'll be getting all sappy thinking about how "wonderful" he is, and she'll be in danger of a relapse. Nice work.

Lazy Girl Hack: Focus on Your Friend's Pain

The point being, you don't need to pretend you loved the guy—that's too ambitious, and would seem about as real as Victoria Beckham's bone structure. Instead, empathize with your friend's feelings. Think about the losses in your life, how you struggled with them, and how you finally got through them. By drawing from your own experiences, you'll show her that not only have you been there—you survived. And she will too. If you do this right, it's barely faking at all. And if you've still got the urge to openly celebrate your friend's emancipation from that a-hole, just remember that he might be back next week. And if you don't play nice now, guess who's going to get the Kim Jong Il treatment later?

PROBLEM

Your Work Wife Gets Promoted and You're Super Jealous

So, your best friend in the office has landed that coveted promotion and you're truly happy for her, really you are. You'd just be a teeny bit happier if you'd also gotten a (slightly better) promotion . . .

Envy is a very ugly—but very common—aspect of friendship. We women especially hate feeling it, because our bonds are strong, meaningful, and unrelated to football. So how can you love this woman while simultaneously wishing you could slither into her house and steal her life like some nasty, heartless Grinchette?

I could go on and on about how jealousy stems from insecurity and a lack of fulfillment in our own lives, but instead I will break it down with a simple analogy. After looking at her piece of cake, your piece of cake is looking pretty crappy. The more you focus on her cake, the more you start to feel deprived and resentful. Eating cake with her then becomes more painful than fun, even though she's always been your favorite person to eat cake with. But it's not about her cake; it's about your cake.

Ugh! If all this talk about cake just makes you want to go emotional eat in the corner, here are some super low-key ways to not let your jealousy ruin your relationship with your friend. After all, who's going to roll her eyes with you when your boss says something stupid or head out to happy hour with you when you have an early conference call the next morning if not your work wife!

Lazy Girl Hack: Admit Your Jealousy

The first step to faking happiness when you're secretly jealous is to at least be honest with yourself. Admit to yourself that you are feeling insanely envious, even though you wish you weren't. We women tend to lie to ourselves about jealousy, because it's such an icky emotion to feel. But if you deny your own feelings, they will come out sideways on you. Trust me. Women who repress their jealousy are the same ones who blurt out remarks like "It's great you could get that promotion—even at your age!" or "He's a real keeper—it's so awesome that he's open-minded about weight" or "I thought hot tubs were just for swingers." Don't be that girl—you'll end up without any friends to be jealous of, and finding new friends is just too much work.

Lazy Girl Hack: Lie, Lie, Lie!

Okay, so once you've been honest with yourself about your jealousy, the next step is to be completely and utterly dishonest with your friend about it. You absolutely *cannot* tell her about this feeling, or sulk about it, or project anything other than total support and joy for her. You will need to make your best effort to make sure your voice does not convey tones of bitterness, sadness, or annoyance. At the same time, you don't want to sound like a sugarcoated, five-exclamation-points phony, because she will see right through that. The fact is, if you're close, your friend probably already knows that this is killing you. And she will appreciate your summoning up your support and love even more.

Lazy Girl Hack: Take Inventory

So, you've faced your yucky feeling and you've lied until your pants literally caught on fire. Congratulations! After you've extinguished your fiery, ashen pants, the next step is to figure out why your friend's good fortune hurt so much. This means taking a long, hard look at your own life and figuring out what's missing. Do you want more responsibility at work? Do you need a career change? You need to answer these questions for yourself and then make life changes accordingly. Do whatever it takes so you won't be blindsided by jealousy again. Then politely thank the Academy, your mom, and sweet baby Jesus for the friendship Oscar you've won (for Best Supporting, naturally!). Then casually stroll down your imaginary red carpet in your scorched pants.

PROBLEM

You Forgot to Make a Dinner Reservation and Need One ASAP

There's a hot new restaurant in town, and this place is exclusive. You and your friends have been talking about it for months and you found out this morning that you were supposed to make a reservation. Like months ago when you first started hearing about the place. Needless to say, you procrastinated and then forgot completely, so that didn't happen.

Now you have to get your lazy butt in gear and find a way to get in for dinner. It's important to remember that dinner reservations cannot be acquired simply through good looks and personality; once again, you're going to have to fake it.

Lazy Girl Hack: Know the Reservationist

One person who has a great deal of power to make or break your restaurant dream is the reservationist. This is a harried, multitasking individual who is telephonically manipulated and abused all day. Yet this individual also has the ability to squeeze people in as needed. It doesn't sound as cool as knowing the chef, but it's more likely to actually work. Here's why.

Sadly, the whole "I know the chef" or "I know the owner" thing has gotten a bit played out—restaurants have become savvy to this game. In fact, it's generally assumed that if you really are a friend of the chef, you'd just call your pal directly, and he or she would get you on the list.

If you pretend to know the reservationist, though, you *are* calling your "friend" directly. It's still a risky venture, but it's less expected than the "chef" routine. The reservationist is used to being treated like someone to brush past, an insignificant peon. She'll probably be surprised to be called by name and addressed personally. Plus, it takes supersized cojones to call and say, "I know you," when you don't.

Lazy Girl Hack: Play the Name Game

If you are determined to pretend to know the owner or chef of a restaurant, it's crucial that you do your basic homework on the person you're pretending to know. For example, according to a classic piece by Kim Severson, former food writer for the *San Francisco Chronicle*, reservation seekers frequently called Café Kati, a popular restaurant at the time, claiming to know "Kati." Well, they may as well have claimed to know Santa Claus, because "Kati" didn't exist—the name was a combination of the two owners' names. This is just sloppy work, my friends! If you are really that eager to get into a restaurant, you should be willing to do at least some basic online research. If you aren't sure about the details, don't elaborate!

Lazy Girl Hack: Become a Food Blogger

This is possibly your best bet for getting into your coveted dining spot. Yes, I know, there are probably more food bloggers in existence today than dust mites, but you're going to do it right.

To start with, you're going to show up in person to make your reservation. This often gives a prospective diner a leg up anyway, since the phone lines are likely as tied up as a radio station having a call-in contest.

The next step is to get some press credentials. There are several organizations online that allow bloggers to acquire press credentials for a fee. Some of these even have official-looking photo IDs for extra authenticity. Then put on some professional, polished-looking clothes and show up with your press credentials, saying you'd like to write a review of the restaurant. Keep your cool if they say yes—no gushing. Save it for the review you'll put up on your faux blog.

PROBLEM

You Bump Into Someone You've Been Avoiding and Have to Play Nice

You should have known better than to allow yourself to be fixed up on a date with Great Aunt Louise's friend's grandson, especially after hearing what a "clean-cut young man" he is. In your experience, "clean-cut young man" either means (a) boring-as-sin alphabetizer of DMV surcharge documents whose idea of fun is combing the beach with a metal detector; (b) serial killer who has cleared space in his freezer for you; or (c) all of the above.

Well, at least the guy didn't kill you—yet—but after one date, you are absolutely positive you never want to see him again and you're seriously thinking about putting more effort into finding your own dates from now on. You haven't exactly gotten around to spelling this out, but you would think that your refusal to take or return any of his fifty-seven phone calls might have implied this. However, as good as he might be at detecting metal, this guy is not very good at detecting "no."

It's too bad you don't have a device that can detect him, because if you did, you never would've ventured to the grocery store today. Because who should you see, weirdly weighing individual eggs on the produce scale, but Mr. Not-So-Right. At the very moment you try to duck, he spots you and makes a beeline in your direction. You make a desperate attempt to run, but he's stunningly fast and agile, and he blocks your way with his cart. You are so busted and instantly regret not ending things when your date went south.

Lazy Girl Hack: Don't Act Guilty

The truth is, you've been totally avoiding this person, and now you've been caught. But the last I checked, avoiding a person who's totally annoying and can't take "no" for an answer is not a punishable crime. So ease up on your guilt! It's great that you're a nice person and you don't like to hurt people, but sometimes there's really no other choice. This guy already has you where he wants you (literally trapped by his grocery cart) and if you let him guilt you, he'll also have you where he wants you psychologically. See, people who glom onto other people—I call them "social parasites"—are a very hardy breed. They *know* that other people don't want them around, and they've developed elaborate ways to force themselves into your life anyway. Guilt is one of their key survival techniques. If you act too flustered and give way to guilt, he will be holding all the cards.

Lazy Girl Hack: Be Busy, Busy

One of the first things you should say is that you've been really busy lately, whether or not it is true. You've been busy avoiding him, haven't you? If you want, you can even pull the guilt-reversal technique, wherein you say, "Yes, I've had a family emergency that has kept me busy." This turns the guilt right back on him! How dare he act so confrontational, given what you've been dealing with? Another great option is the "personal crisis." This works on a few levels: It takes the guilt off you, and also draws a clear line between your personal life and this guy. If he tries to get more information out of you, very politely say that you'd rather not discuss it. A lot of us "nice girls" don't know the line between being courteous and having no boundaries at all. You can do one without doing the other.

Lazy Girl Hack: Avoid CAGE

Another pitfall "nice girls" run into, when confronted by someone they've been avoiding, is pressure to make future plans. You're trapped, you're guilty and embarrassed, and he's saying, "When can we hang out?" You feel as though the only way you can escape is to agree to a future plan. But this will only perpetuate the vicious cycle of Calls, Avoidance, Guilt, and Entrapment (CAGE for short; yes, I made that up). Say something vague, like, "It would be nice to see you again (a lie, yes), but I'm swamped right now." This is unlikely to slake the insatiable appetite of the social parasite, but unless he wants to look totally deranged in public, he has to accept it. All that's left is to say, "It was nice to see you," and run.

PROBLEM

You're Invited to a Fancy Dinner, but Don't Know a Salad Fork from a Soup Spoon

So you've been invited to a large extended-family dinner celebrating a milestone birthday for Great Aunt Millie. You're no stranger to eating out (let's be honest, it's way easier than cooking for yourself), but this dinner is going to be over-the-top fancy schmancy. You're nervous because not only are you a natural klutz with food and silverware, you haven't a clue about the weird encoded rules of table manners. (*How many tines on a salad fork again?*) It seems grossly unfair how easily you can accidentally be offensive without meaning one bit of harm. Seriously, your elbows are just comfortable there! If you don't have the time or the inclination to do some serious table manner research, these dinnertime hacks will save the day. Or at least dinner.

Lazy Girl Hack: Wait!

According to www.quickanddirtytips.com, patience is a very important virtue of table manners. This especially applies to being considerate of your fellow diners. For example, you should wait to sit down until you've helped those who need help being seated. You should wait to take bread from a breadbasket until you've offered some to others. You should wait to begin eating until the host or hostess has started to eat. Oh, and you should wait until you've finished chewing to answer a question someone has asked you. If answering means treating the whole table to an insider's view of your partially masticated mushroom ravioli, postponing your reply is not considered rude. However, if someone is choking on a chicken bone and you know the Heimlich, waiting would be sort of terrible.

Lazy Girl Hack: Know about Elbows

If you're a bit of a table manners novice, you might wonder, "What is so horrible about elbows?" They are just innocuous joints, maybe a little on the pointy side but not offensive in any way. It's not like people are outside sticking their elbows into the dirt or spreading elbow STDs (I hope)! So why is there this bizarre rule about no elbows on the table? One theory, according to www.chowhound.com, is that if your elbows are on the table, you're probably hunched over your food in a way that makes you look like a crazed Neanderthal. In order to avoid this hunched-over posture, imagine what would happen if the table were suddenly whisked out from under you. Would you fall? That means you're hugging that table a little bit too hard. If you love that food, set it free. If it comes back to you, you definitely ate too much.

You Know You're a Lazy Girl When . . .
You view paint parties as kindergarten art classes with wine.

Lazy Girl Hack: Study Up on Forks, Spoons, Knives, and Napkins

Okay, now on to the tricky part—silverware and napkins. You've been using this stuff since you were a kid, but there's a difference between pretending your spoon is a choo-choo train and properly using silverware for its designated purpose. And for whatever reason, fancy schmancy dinner party types like to set up sadistic tests for the rest of us by having a zillion different identical-looking implements lined up together like multiple-choice questions. Trying to choose the right one is like MacGyver trying to choose the right wire to snip—one disarms the bomb, the other . . . blows the effing place sky-high.

It's a snobby little test, to be sure, but there's an excellent cheat sheet. The silverware is usually used from the outside in. So the first fork on the outside should be used for the salad, the first spoon for the soup, etc. Of course, if there's something truly bizarre on the outside of your lineup, like a melon baller or plastic beach shovel, don't start with those. *Everyone* knows plastic beach shovels are for dessert!

PROBLEM

You Have to Pretend to Like Someone You Completely Hate

Okay, I can just picture all those sanctimonious, high-and-mighty types wagging their fingers and saying, "Why would you ever need to fake a friendship when you can't stand someone? That's like lying, and lying is *wrong* . . . "

Yeah, yeah, yeah. Sometimes, it's just easier to fake even the sacred bonds of friendship than it is to have some awkward confrontation with someone. Maybe your abrasive boss has taken a shine to you and wants to be your BFF. Maybe there's an endearingly nerdy, awkward friend-of-a-friend who worships the ground you walk on. Or maybe your mom has this terrible idea that since you're an adult now, the two of you should be "girlfriends." The list goes on and on.

The reality is, most fake friendships are temporary. Either they grow on you and graduate to real friendship, or they fade mercifully away. Until then, there's no need to crush this person's spirit. Think of all your mom has done for you!

Lazy Girl Hack: Fake It on Social Media

If ever there was a place meant for fake friendship to grow and flourish while barely touching the real world, it is social media. Social networking is an ideal place to carry out "friendships" that you don't necessarily need to become friendships. Make sure you're friends with your faux girlfriend online, and try to give her as much virtual love and attention as you can manage. Give thumbs up to any of her statuses that you can remotely stand, share her posts, and comment on any pictures of universally great things, like kittens or chocolate cake. Try your best to keep this friendship as confined to the virtual realm as you can. In this way, you can be sitting at your computer thinking, "I can't stand you, you crazy bleep!" while typing something more like "Yay! You go, girl!" Maintaining this contradiction is much easier in the virtual world than in real life, so do your best to keep it unreal. If your "friend" tries to extend this connection into real life, you should either try to politely decline invitations to get together, or make those real-world hangouts memorably bad. Show up with a disgusting cold, maybe, or whine about your PMS the entire time. After a few of these, she will begin to think: *Social media friendship equals good; real life friendship equals horrible and potentially germ-spreading.*

Lazy Girl Hack: Keep It at the Office

Ah, work friendships. With the right person, they can be a saving grace for those hours spent within the cubicle walls. With the wrong person, they feel like a second full-time job. Yet there are circumstances, usually dictated by subtle and horrible office politics, in which you must "make nice" with someone who couldn't make nice if someone handed her the recipe. This is unfortunate, but the point is this: eight hours is a long time. And really, those eight hours should be more than enough time to have to contribute to a faux friendship. Try to limit your after-work interactions with your faux friend to workplace group activities, such as happy hours or book clubs. These activities will still fall under the heading of "workplace," and will be buffered by other coworkers. You should *not* have to go with your boss to get bikini waxes or to a Justin Bieber concert with her and her tween daughter. So feel free to politely decline invitations that feel too personal and just plain weird. If necessary, use your significant other as an excuse. If you don't have a significant other, I'm not necessarily saying you should go out and get one just to keep this lady at bay, but . . . you know, if you wanted to, I'm not going to stop you.

PROBLEM

You Have to Spend the Holidays with Your Family and It Gets Awkward

You love your life: You've worked hard to get out of your hometown, establish a career, buy a house, and make great friends. You're a confident, intelligent, accomplished woman who works hard, is the life of the party, and is deserving of love and respect. You're attractive. You haven't had a bad perm for literally years.

These are just some of the affirmations you will need to say to yourself in order to survive dragging yourself home—or even to an isolated family function—for the holidays.

It's always the same: At first, you look forward to getting there, telling them about the recent developments in your life, relating to them as a fellow adult. Then you get there, and as far as they're concerned, you're still the twelve-year-old in the peach-colored eighties glasses and a sweatshirt with a wolf on it. They listen to you pretending to be a grownup for about ten minutes, then your cousin Jimmy gives you an Indian rope burn and calls you "Spazz," his old nickname for you. Your dad asks if you've let your car run out of gas lately (a bad habit from your youth), and Aunt Marie asks if you're *still single* as if she were asking if you *still have malaria*.

Some things never change. But wait—*you've* changed! Why can't your family see that? But since yelling "I'm a grown-up!" at your family won't actually make them see you as an adult, here are some slightly less crazy, less confrontational ways to make it through.

Lazy Girl Hack: Bring Souvenirs from Your Real Life

Families suffer from a kind of collective poor vision—all they can see are the designated family roles they established years ago. So if you're the family nerd, the loser, or the spazz, their tendency will be to see that—even if you have three doctoral degrees and have won the Nobel Prize.

One strategy I find useful when visiting family is to bring a souvenir from your *real* life. This can be anything that reminds you of your current life and who you really are, which is very different from the outdated memories your family might still maintain. Best of all is a human souvenir, like a good friend who doesn't want to see their family, either. If you can't bring a person, try to have a friend on hand to talk to on the phone or by text, just to give you reminders that you are understood, valued, and highly regarded as a fully adult human being. Or, if you're in a pinch, just bring your Nobel Prize along for the trip.

Lazy Girl Hack: Don't Try to "Sell" Yourself

One trap grown children fall into during the holidays is to try to "sell" the new, mature version of themselves to their family members. This isn't necessary or helpful. Families are quite resistant to updating their ideas of who you are now. If you were a little kid with pigtails, Great Aunt Edna might not be able to accommodate your current identity as a political activist and roller derby queen. No matter. It's not important. You don't need to convince Great Aunt Edna of anything, no more than she needs to convince you that her nose hair is not a living creature.

Lazy Girl Hack: Try Not to Be Hurt

It's possible that someone in your family might say something hurtful about your current life. Maybe Uncle George will say, "Well, I thought you had more sense than to try to open a *dog bakery* during a recession. What is a dog bakery? Do you bake dogs?" Or "Hmm, so your boyfriend is a musician. Does that mean he's unemployed?" Or "Oh, so you're a vegetarian. Doesn't that kind of conflict with your dog bakery?" There is really no end to the things family members might try to say, especially if your lifestyle seems threatening or opposed to their way of life. I would advise returning to the mantra that "My life is good. This isn't my real life. This is a bizarre suspended reality known as the holidays." And it will be over, and you'll survive it. You want to project a quiet dignity, a sort of "I'm past all your nonsense" aura. It really is a wonderful life. Honest!

PROBLEM

Your Friends Hate Reality TV, but It's Your Guilty Pleasure

Here is a rough transcript of a recent conversation between you and your friends. (Sorry I've been secretly recording your conversations. Please don't sue.)

Friend 1: "OMG, have you seen that show about the former eighties child stars who all live together on that boat and are dared to eat each other's disgustingly cooked meals in order to win the heart of the eligible dolphin fisherman bachelor? I think it's called *Celebrity Bachelorette Bad Chef: High Seas Challenge* or something."

Friend 2: "That show is *so* stupid, so demeaning to women—and the food?! Repulsive. And who wants to marry a dolphin fisherman, anyway? Dolphins are the smartest animals around. That guy's an idiot."

You: "Yeah, it's um . . . really bad . . . That's . . . a bad show, all right."

Friend 1 and Friend 2, in horrified unison: "Oh my God, you like it!" (pointing, laughing) "She likes it!"
[You cry. End of scene.]

This scene could have been prevented. Yes, you *are* secretly intrigued by the crazy antics—and questionable seaweed and jellyfish recipes—of those former eighties celebrity bachelorettes at sea. And you *do* happen to think that dolphin fisherman Eric *is* kind of dreamy. But the truth is, some reality shows just aren't cool to like. And why should you be the one getting pointed and laughed at?

Don't give up your guilty pleasure! But don't give up your social life either.

Lazy Girl Hack: Know the Jargon

If you want to sound convincing about not liking that reality show, or any other reality show you might secretly love, you have to talk the talk. You don't want to critique it on its entertainment value (because we all know reality shows are ridiculously entertaining), but rather on its impact on society. You see, everyone gets their feathers ruffled about the use of the word "reality" to describe these shows, taking this as a sign that our "real" world is bound for hell in the proverbial handbasket. It's so silly, because *everyone* knows these shows contain as much actual reality as Heidi Montag's boobs. They're like the modern equivalent of soap operas, except with fewer comas. So this maneuver will be a double fake: You have to fake not liking something that is, itself, a fake. Say things like "It's such a pathetic commentary on our society that . . . " and trail off and shake your head disapprovingly. Someone will pick up that thread for you, I guarantee. Another popular refrain among reality show haters is that the stars are "famous for being famous." You can always sarcastically say, "I love it that you don't actually have to *do* anything or have any *talent* to become a star." Of course, some reality stars might argue that eating rat testicles while riding a unicycle is, indeed, doing something.

Lazy Girl Hack: Like the Show "Ironically"

One coping mechanism that is very popular among conflicted, closeted reality TV show fans is the liberal use of "irony." As in, fake irony. It's very common to hide behind irony when liking things that are terribly embarrassing to like. So rather than displaying flat-out sincerity, which is the equivalent of showing up at work naked, we cloak our love in eye-rolling, protective-irony wear. Say, "Yeah, *Celebrity Bachelorette Bad Chef: High Seas Challenge* is just so *entertaining*." By saying "entertaining" in that type of eye-rolling way you're acknowledging that you know the show is stupid and you don't really like it–like it, you just watch it because it's kind of cool to like things you don't like. Everyone will nod vigorously, and some might say, "Me too!"

Next, follow up with a mocking commentary of the cast, something like "Did you see that episode where dolphin fisherman Eric says he's looking for his soul mate to eat dolphin burgers with forever? Total *freak*!" Never mind that when you watched it, you solemnly mouthed to the TV, "I'll eat dolphin burgers with you, Eric," and touched his face on the screen. It's like when you secretly loved that nerdy boy in seventh grade, but disowned him in front of the cool girls. Be prepared for a bit of irony-sickness.

PROBLEM

Your Friend Calls You, but You Don't Really Want to Talk

We live in the age of multitasking—people close business deals while pumping breast milk, scrolling social media, and trading their roommates for kayaks on Craigslist. This is especially true when someone calls you to talk on the phone.

I mean, who actually wants to talk when you can just text each other? It's not like you can send emojis when you're actually speaking to one another. And who has the time or the mental capacity to just sit on the couch and talk to someone for hours on end? No one. That's who. And fortunately, despite being a lazy girl, you can be the queen of multitasking and make it through that phone call with your street cred intact.

Lazy Girl Hack: Acknowledge That There's a Lot Going On in the Background

One great way to do a zillion things while talking on the phone without a smidgen of guilt is to just tell your friend that you have a lot going on in your house. Maybe your dog is barking in the background. Take the time to yell at him. Feel like watching TV? Just lie about what that big explosion on the screen was. Maybe a transformer blew up the street. The good thing about that is that you can rush off the phone because there's a chance your battery will die.

If you're lucky, your friend will be distracted too. For example, maybe she's a mom. No one in the world, no matter what technology they have at their fingertips, could possibly be as distracted as a mom whose kids are present. You can sit there and check your Twitter page while murmuring "uh-huh" and "okay" and your friend will be permitted approximately six words of adult conversation before she screams, "Jayden! Put that down!" or "Sophia! Share with your brother!" You'll then hear a garbled exchange with the offending child, and she'll return to you with a sigh. "Sorry," she will say.

It's brilliant! You've been watching a YouTube video of a kitten riding on a turtle's back the whole conversation, and *she's* apologizing to you! Well played!

Lazy Girl Hack: Mix and Match

Regarding work or urgent friend calls, my advice is to mix a mental task with a physical task. If you do a menial physical job while talking, you're still leaving a large chunk of your brain open to the conversation. So, to review: a conversation about your friend's horrible husband while doing laundry equals good; a conversation about your friend's horrible husband while preparing a grueling work presentation and bidding for an antique Chewbacca action figure equals bad. Likewise, a work conference call while making salad equals good; a work conference call while emailing your BFF about her ovulation-timing difficulties equals bad.

PROBLEM

You Told Your Friend You Were Too Sick to Go Out, but You Went Out Anyway

Remember the time you called in sick to your friend's stupid paint night with a high fever and flu, and then you ran into her at your local bar later on that night? First there was that sickening feeling in the pit of your stomach as you said hello to her, then there was your sad, awkward attempt at casual conversation, then you realized that you had to figure out how to get out of the situation.

Don't feel bad. Everyone occasionally goes places they're not supposed to be when they're supposed to be home sick. And it's not your fault that you didn't want to go to a stupid paint night. Here are some hacks to get you out of it with your friendship intact.

Lazy Girl Hack: Always Order Jell-O Shots

This is a piece of advice I never thought I'd have occasion to give, but there it is. I should preface this by saying that if you absolutely need to hit the bar while you're supposed to be home sick, go to an out-of-the-way location. Taking this simple step can go a long way toward saving your skin.

But once you are out and about, and you're drinking either way, Jell-O shots are the way to go. "What's that?" you might ask. "Jell-O shots? They're the most juvenile, ridiculous frat party drink in the world! Why should I order them?"

Hello . . . Does no one remember when you were a kid and you had an upset stomach, and Jell-O was one of the few things you could keep down without puking? Well, if you get caught out on the town when you're supposed to be sick, that Jell-O could be your saving grace. The only thing better would be chicken soup shots, and they don't exist (I checked). Say, "Well I just wanted a little fresh air, but all my stomach can tolerate is this Jell-O" (wince stoically). There is *no need* to tell them that your stomach-sparing Jell-O is spiked with ninety-proof rum. However, if said rum should make you sick enough to vomit during your interaction with your friend, the whole thing could come full circle in a beautiful way.

Lazy Girl Hack: Be Prepared to Go with It

Maybe your friend's paint night is on a Saturday night, and you said you were sick on Friday. Then, on Saturday afternoon, who should you run into at the mall but Ms. Party Host? She smiles and says, "Oh, wow—are you feeling better? Does this mean you'll be able to come tonight?"

Well, I'm sorry to tell you this, but you've managed to get yourself caught in a little trap here. The lure of Saturday afternoon shopping led you to take this wanton risk, and now the steely snare of the trap just clamped down on your leg. In order to save yourself, you may need to gnaw that leg off.

Just put your fake in reverse and say, "I was going to call you later. Yes, I'm feeling much better. What can I bring?" Learn from this experience—you took a gamble, and you lost. Hope that sale at the Gap was worth it!

You Know You're a Lazy Girl When . . .
You feel relieved when your friends cancel plans because it means you can put on your pajamas and spend the night at home on the couch.

Lazy Girl Hack: Go Bare

If you do feel compelled to go to a risky place while you're supposed to be sick, drop your vanity and skip the makeup. Leaving the house without makeup is one of the very best tricks of the fake-sick trade. You know how you diligently apply your makeup each day so you can resemble a halfway normal-looking human? Just do the opposite. The fact is that most women without their makeup look genuinely sick. If you go out sans makeup, your naked face will do most of the lying for you. People will take one look at you and want to feed you Jell-O shots!

PROBLEM

Your Friends Keep Setting You Up, but You Hate It

Your friends might mean well, but things usually don't end well when people "mean well." The phrase "mean well" is nothing but a preface to disastrous behavior committed with nice intentions. In fact, just FYI, if someone ever says to you, "I know you mean well," you can expect a big "but" and an explanation of what you did that sort of sucked.

Okay, now that I've finished that rant, let's talk about your well-meaning friends. The trouble is, they set you up with each and every male human who crosses their paths: their weird brothers, guys they rejected, the undertakers at their grandmas' funerals. They set you up with their secretly married plumbers, and their secretly gay yoga instructors. You're pretty sure they're one step away from setting you up with their dogs and their robotic vacuum cleaners.

It's gotten pretty insulting, actually. Clearly, one friend thinks you're not above dating a bald, sixty-five-year-old taxidermist she found selling stuffed alligators at a roadside stand, and another imagines you might be fine with a convicted car thief who "only has a few more months" before his release.

You can't take this anymore. Bad dates are exhausting (let's be honest, even good dates are exhausting) and you've had enough. Something has to change, and that something is your relationship status. You have to fake a date—and an amazing one—ASAP.

Lazy Girl Hack: Get a Text Boyfriend

To plant the initial seed of your new relationship status, you need to start getting texts from your fake man. To this end, there are a few "fake boyfriend" services available online. For a set fee, you can get a set number of sweet, attentive, and charming texts from this faux beau per week. If your friends ask who this mysterious texting man is, you can say, "He's somebody special I've been seeing," and make a face that is both enigmatic and quite pleased. If they ask whether it's serious, you can lay the groundwork by saying, "Let's just put it this way: I don't think I'm going to need to be set up on any blind dates anytime soon."

Lazy Girl Hack: Have a Long-Distance Love

Here's one problem with the text boyfriend—if this guy is important enough to call a halt to all fix-ups, your friends will probably expect him to become an in-person fixture. And unless you know some guy who is willing to play that role on an ongoing basis, your best faking option is probably a long-distance relationship.

Say you met this guy on a work trip, or visiting a relative, or even online if necessary. He'll have to live far enough away to justify his infrequent visits. Or, you can say that when he does manage to come to town, he wants to maximize his time alone with you. Aw, I like this guy already!

If you can't get a friend or coworker to pose as your man for an evening, what you will probably need to do is hire an amateur actor. Often, you can find guys who do singing telegrams, or even strippers, who will happily take the gig. Offer to pay him the same amount he would get for an "event" to pretend to be your boyfriend. Surely, he can show up to your friend's party, look handsome, and answer a few basic questions. If you happen to hire a stripper, remind him that he does not need to take off his clothes. Although if he does, that might put an end to all the questions!

Lazy Girl Hack: Be Ready to Dump Him

Yes, this fake man is serving a valuable purpose for you right now, by keeping your friends' hideous setups at bay. But should you meet someone special, you need to be willing to dump this dude immediately, even if your friends love him. You need to tell them that this guy cheated on you with a clown prostitute. And got her pregnant. And gave you gonorrhea—whatever it takes to get out of your fake relationship and into a real one.

PART 3

Finding Love and Having Sex

There's something about the dating scene right now that just seems exhausting. It's a lot of work to create an online dating profile, suffer through bad date after bad date, and figure out how to escape from that bad date and never see the person ever again. And then, when you finally manage to find someone who sets your heart aflutter, you have to deal with his friends, and his family, and figuring out how to fake an orgasm when he wants to make you so happy but all you want to do is finish things up so you can lie down. So yes, dating, finding love, and having sex are intense, but they're worth it . . . especially when you have the lazy girl hacks in this part to get you off on the right foot.

PROBLEM

You're Too Lazy to Spend Time on Your Online Dating Profile, but Want to Meet a Guy

If there is one thing you cannot stand, it's long walks on the beach. Not only are they too freaking long, but the sand gets in your hair, you run the risk of cutting your feet on shells, and the water's freezing! And on top of all that, they make you a total cliché on your online dating profile. Frankly, you'd rather take a long walk off a short pier (note to self: they really need to start making longer piers for distance walkers).

Look, you're complicated and interesting—hardly cookie-cutter (although you do love cookie dough). So when it's time to create your online dating profile, you want to include stuff that will reflect your uniqueness and spark. However, you don't want to cross the line—too many of those "Look at me!" profiles get a flurry of short-term attention, a few dates, and then nothing. You want to be noticed in a good way, in a way that will last—because you can't build a life, a home, and a family on a bunch of casual dates.

So since the last thing you want to spend a ton of time on is your dating profile, here are some hacks to make it easy. Check them out and reap the benefits!

Lazy Girl Hack: Be Specific

When it comes to describing yourself in an online dating profile, the opposite of "boring" is "specific." What do you think when you read in someone's profile that they "like music," "enjoy the outdoors," and "love to laugh"? Do you think anything at all in the midst of the temporary coma you've slipped into? I know I don't! I have never met a human being who doesn't at least occasionally love music, laughter, and the outdoors. These descriptors, therefore, say next to nothing about you, and are as good as wasted. I think I might be more intrigued by a person who *hates* music and laughter. At least this would make him unforgettable in a bad way. I wouldn't want to date him, but I'd remember him. I'd tell my friends, "Remember that guy who hated music and laughter?" And we'd all laugh, which would be even funnier because that would be something that guy would totally hate.

You Know You're a Lazy Girl When . . .

The only "long walks on the beach" you want any part of are the ones on cute guy's dating profile.

It really doesn't take that much more effort to narrow your focus to something more specific. You could say, "Likes Inuit throat singing music," or "Loves to laugh when other people trip and fall," or "Enjoys outdoor urination." Even if what you say isn't exactly the most alluring thing ever, it's definitely going to be better than a generic catchall. Review your profile, and wherever you see yourself generalizing, kick it up a notch. If you find yourself saying things like "enjoys new experiences," "values loyalty," or "loves life," ask yourself one question: Is there anyone on the planet who *doesn't* like the thing you're describing? If the answer is no, you're probably speaking in clichés. You can do better than that!

Lazy Girl Hack: Be Picture Realistic

Okay, one thing we know is that when it comes to seeking out a mate, whether for life or for the night, looks do matter. And have you ever clicked on a profile where you couldn't see what the guy looked like? Of course not! So you definitely do want to include at least one or two good, flattering photos of yourself with your profile. By "flattering" I don't mean "deceptive." The picture should be relatively recent, and be a realistic depiction of what you look like. For example, if you've shaved your head or gained 100 pounds, it's not wise to post a picture from before such a change occurred.

PROBLEM

You're Just Not That Into Him, but Don't Know How to Let Him Know

WTF?! Could this date possibly get any worse? First, the guy shows up at the restaurant wearing a tank top, skinny jeans, and fluorescent green Crocs. You try to look past these heinous fashion crimes as you imbibe a pre-dinner glass of wine. As the alcohol enters your system, you start to enjoy his sense of humor, which isn't excellent but at least exists. He also has a nice smile, and earns points by saying he doesn't really go clubbing anymore—he's more of a "homebody" these days. It's almost enough to make you forgive the Crocs.

Then your eyes scan up from the offending foam resin shoes to reveal a disturbing accessory—an electronic ankle bracelet. Before you even have time to ask about this, he tells you that he "escaped" his house arrest to come out on this date, and that if he doesn't get home soon, he's probably going to jail. Couldn't you give him a ride home? He'd love to continue the date at his house.

Again, WTF?! Although this is certainly the most creative approach any guy has taken to lure you back to his house, it's also the worst. Especially since you haven't even ordered dinner and he's not making a move to pick up the drink tab. Meanwhile, the clock is running out on House Arrest Cinderella here. And those Crocs are a far cry from magic slippers. A "homebody," indeed!

Now, you don't want to tell this guy that you're having a horrible time and he's the worst date ever. He's wearing an ankle bracelet, for God's sake! And if you hate anything, it's confrontation. What's a lazy girl to do?

Lazy Girl Hack: Stay Drama Free

Okay, so it goes without saying that you're never going to see this man again, except maybe on a "wanted" poster. You just want to end the night with a minimum of drama. As you walk him to the cab you plan to put him in, try to say something sort of nice, since these are hopefully the last words you will ever utter to him. Feel free to employ some humor. Say, "Well, it was a short date, but certainly an adventure. It was nice to meet you." If he tries to get you to commit to another date, you can say something vague, like, "Well, things are looking really busy right now . . . I'm sure I'll see you around." This is a white lie to get you out of this situation. And hey, you might see him again sometime, when you are required to testify against him at his parole violation hearing.

Lazy Girl Hack: Get Rid of Guilt!

It is very important that you not reveal any guilt over the fact that you hated this date and never want to see this person again. Guilt is the kiss of death when you are trying to lose a loser. If he senses you are a little bit of a pushover, he will try to play that for all it's worth. You don't owe this guy anything. You can mention a few positive aspects of the date—were there any? Oh, right, you did like his sense of humor there for a minute, unless it was just the wine. But don't say, "I liked your sense of humor"; that's too personal. Cite one funny story he told and say, "Oh, I liked that story of your experience bartering cigarettes and shanks with your friends, ha-ha."

Lazy Girl Hack: Avoid the Kiss of Death

If guilt is the kiss of death, then a kiss is the kiss of worse-than-death, and the only thing worse than death would be to get stuck in a relationship with this guy. Under no circumstances are you obligated to kiss this person. You can be nice, mildly complimentary, and generically polite, but you don't need to make contact with his lips. If he tries to go in for the kiss, you're going to have to turn your head and give him the infamous mouth full of hair. Honestly, if you've suffered through a bad date, you should not further need to suffer through a bad kiss too. I would suggest politely shaking his hand. You can allow a peck only if there seems to be absolutely no way to avoid it in a socially acceptable way. Just remember that it's a kiss goodbye.

PROBLEM

You're on a Horrible Date and Need to Cut It Short

You're on a date that started out iffy, then progressed to not so good, and then took a rapid nosedive to absolutely horrific. This guy's versions of "compliments" to you are that he "likes a girl with meat on her bones," "likes a woman who's not too intellectual," and "likes a girl who's not so pretty she's a snob." Despite the fact that his compliments have more backhand than a Serena Williams tennis game, he's now pawing ineptly at you like a raccoon trying to knock over a trash can. Oh, and apparently he likes a girl who picks up the check too.

He's proposed the idea that you hang out and have some more drinks, and maybe go back to his place, but you're pretty sure you'd rather be skinned alive. This isn't just a typical bad date. It's the worst date you've ever been on and you don't need to put up with this crap, not even for another minute. You need to hack this date . . . and fast!

Lazy Girl Hack: Get an Emergency Text

Back in the days before cell phones, people had to rely on the most archaic methods for getting out of bad dates, like having a friend actually show up at the date location with some "emergency." Imagine how difficult that was back in the days before cars existed—the date intervener had to hitch up the horse and buggy and drive for days, by which time the date was probably over. It's no wonder so many people in olden days ended up marrying people they hated—no one showed up to get them out of it!

Now, all of our fancy little gadgets make it easier than ever to end a horrendous date. In particular, our cell phones are little miracles of faux emergency.

You Know You're a Lazy Girl When . . .

You didn't even bother to ghost your ex—you just kind of played dead.

There are a wide variety of options for using your cell phone in this way, ranging from the homemade approach to actual paid services. The most basic approach would be the emergency text, wherein you pretend to get a text calling you away from your date immediately. Of course, you can arrange to get a real text from a participating friend at a set time, or you can text your friend a code requesting this text. You can even show your emergency text to the guy—if it's right there in writing that your grandpa's in the hospital, it can't be a lie, can it? If you do show the guy your friend's text, though, make sure he doesn't see her phone number. She really wouldn't appreciate having this freak calling her, either!

Lazy Girl Hack: There's an App . . .

Yes, we have reached a point in our civilization where we're simultaneously more technologically savvy and more socially inept than ever. It makes sense, then, that at this juncture we would have at our disposal services whereby we can pay to have a date-interrupting phone call made to our cell phones.

There are actually several different apps out there, including Phony Call and Smart Fake Call, that you can use to put a horrible date out of its misery. You can arrange to get a work-related phone call, a request from a friend to bail him out of jail, or an emergency summons to the hospital. One service even lets you get a phone call from a famous person, which will show up on your caller ID! Why would you want to stick around this weirdo when you have celebrities to see?

PROBLEM

You Texted Your New Guy and Immediately Regret It

So you just started dating this guy, and from what you can tell so far, he's pretty awesome. You've only been on a few dates, but you've had some unforgettable kisses and some fun conversations. He's handsome, smart, entertaining, seemingly stable—all of that. Right now, you are smitten.

You're not going to be seeing him for a while, though, because he's away visiting family out of state. The absence is just making your heart grow fonder, and you want to take advantage of the distance to send him some fun, flirty little "thinking of you" texts. What you *really* want is to say, "OMG, I love you, I have been trying on your last name all night long, how many children do you want?" but in your experience, this tends to scare guys away. As it is, even your little flirty stuff is a bit risky, since it's so early on and you don't know where you stand. In fact, you immediately overthink your texting, panic, and start to think of how you can excuse your incredibly forward behavior. God forbid he actually knows how you feel about him when it's this early on, right? For this reason, you want to reserve the right to retract your statements in the morning. Therefore, you need to pretend to be just a little bit drunk. If you claim to be drunk, your little lapses into sappiness will actually seem very restrained. You will seem like a very composed, dignified drunk girl—and who doesn't want to date her!

Lazy Girl Hack: Disable Autocorrect

One great way to signify drunkenness while texting is to commit many typographical and spelling errors. You're a whiz at texting, though, so you'd probably have to try really hard to spell things wrong. Or you can just disable autocorrect.

Okay, although autocorrect certainly has the potential to add to the illusion that you are drunk, I'm not sure you would want to make the kinds of mistakes it tends to make. Autocorrect has a very dirty mind, and tends to create typos that are both perverse and embarrassing. So even if it says something a little bit racy, it's probably not going to be a good kind of racy. According to www.damnyouautocorrect.com, you might accidentally find yourself saying that you "need some new penises—mine broke," or that you "love oblong wieners."

Basically, these are funny mistakes, but they might not be the kind of thing you would want to say to a guy you're just getting to know. You could be so embarrassed you might not even be able to face him the next day, as you struggle with your fake hangover.

Lazy Girl Hack: Be a Little More Playful

Really, it's very easy to pretend to be drunk while texting. Because your physical self isn't involved, you don't have to change your tone, you don't have to slur your words, and you don't have to be wobbly when you walk. All you have to do is seem just a little bit less inhibited, and a little bit more honest. If you sense later that he wasn't ready for this level of playfulness or flirtation, you can always retreat by saying you were tipsy, and no harm done. But maybe he will flirt right back—and maybe he will be drunk for real, which will really help. Hey, why not have a drink yourself, while you're at it?

PROBLEM

You're Having Sex and You're Just Not Going to Get There

Like most of us women, I'm sure you've been there—in bed with a guy, waiting for the Big Moment to occur, reaching for it like the brass ring on the merry-go-round, and realizing that it is cruelly eluding you. No matter how long you stay on the ride, it's just not going to be a very "merry" go-round this time.

It could be that you're stressed, or tired, or have your mind on other things (unlike guys, women have trouble enjoying sex when their lives are falling apart all around them—we're weird like that). Or maybe you're with a guy who is so clueless he thinks the "G-spot" is a section of the parking garage at the mall.

Either way, you've missed your window this time, and you're ready to wrap it up and call it a night. But your partner seems to be courteously waiting for your "big finish" before he concludes his business. If he wants a real orgasm, he could be waiting a really long time. It's like he's politely holding the door for you at the supermarket when you haven't even left your house yet. It's enough to make you wish that chivalry were dead.

You definitely don't want to hurt his feelings, but you're pretty much done. Since you don't want him to feel bad, you realize that if you can perform a convincing piece of theater, the two of you could be happily drifting off to dreamland within ten minutes and he'll never be the wiser. It's not exactly Shakespeare, but it could be the role of your lifetime!

Lazy Girl Hack: Be a Porn Star

The truth is, the pornography industry has done a lot of the groundwork in terms of making your guy gullible in this regard. You know how kids become desensitized to movie explosions and shootouts? Well, so do adult men become desensitized to over-the-top, loud moaning, screaming, and "Oh, God" and "Oh, yeah!"-ing. Guys usually watch a lot more porn than women. What might strike you as preposterously overdone may, therefore, seem entirely credible to him. These imaginary scenarios, combined with their natural egos, have led them to think that women really do reach those levels of ecstasy every single time.

You Know You're a Lazy Girl When . . .

You limit your daily exercise to either going to the gym, housecleaning, or sex. Never all three—and rarely housecleaning.

My point is, although I do think it's best not to overact while faking orgasm, you do have a fairly wide range to work with. Do what you are most comfortable doing—this is the best way to make your performance believable.

Lazy Girl Hack: Build Up Gradually

The most convincing fake orgasm is one where you let your "excitement" build up gradually. Allow your breathing to become more irregular and ragged, and let out moans of increasing intensity and volume. If you're not big into the loud moan, that's okay, but just allow yourself to gradually sound more urgent and excited. Remember, this is supposed to be an involuntary thing, so don't make the moans too regular or perfectly timed, or they might seem fake. Another good approach is to close your eyes, since this is often what you'd do if it were real (plus, looking him right in the eye while faking might be too big of a challenge).

Lazy Girl Hack: Reach the Crescendo

As you get closer to your grand finale, allow more and more involuntary reactions to take place. Maybe bite your lip, or tense the muscles in your legs or feet. Your body might twitch a bit (don't overdo this, as might seem like you're having a seizure) or you might call out his name or some other preferred exclamation (not someone else's name, though, okay?). Grabbing onto something, such as a pillow or his hair, is a nice touch to signal your imminent delight. Then give a loud gasp—gasping is good—and maybe a moan if you'd like, letting it last a few seconds, then relax your body. You can laugh, sigh, or kiss him—some bit of punctuation to let him know you're done. What's best is that he probably won't be capable of critical analysis of your performance, because he'll be right behind you with his own big finish.

And even though faking an orgasm isn't taking the lazy way out, it sure beats having to tell your guy that he just couldn't get it done.

PROBLEM

You Hate How Your Guy Dresses, but Can't Tell Him

You don't need a designer-savvy, trend-enslaved hipster for a boyfriend, but it would be nice if your guy could wear a shirt without stains or a cartoon character on it, and pants that do not include a drawstring. (Exception: If your man is a respected pediatric surgeon, and he's wearing cartoon character medical scrubs to put the sick little children at ease, I want you to drop this book and pinch yourself over your dreamlike good luck. Then punch yourself, just for good measure, and don't let me hear you whine about that man's wardrobe ever again.)

If, however, your guy is the standard issue, T-shirt-and-jeans-wearing slob, or if he dresses like it's the eighties—but not in a good way—or if he engages in the practice known as "sagging" (wearing his jeans so low that his underwear are fully visible), you are probably right to be somewhat mortified. We've all dated that guy whose wardrobe makes us want to crawl into a hole and die. Some of us even marry him. The reason this is such a common problem is that men, generally speaking, are clueless about fashion. Our dating options, therefore, are reduced to men whose personal style makes us cringe, or guys whose meticulous metrosexuality makes us suspicious. Pick your poison, ladies, and pretend to love it because there's only so much you can do to change it. And if you do say something and he does agree to change his style, you're going to be the one out there shopping for a new wardrobe with him, and how awful does that sound?

Lazy Girl Hack: Don't Say It!

The one thing you should not do, especially early on in a relationship, is to tell your man that his sense of fashion is horrific. Part of loving a person is accepting some of his imperfections, and if his wardrobe is the worst thing about him, you're probably very lucky. You certainly wouldn't want him pointing out your flaws, would you? Maybe later in the relationship—like when you're both eighty—you can tell him he dresses terribly. By then, you'll probably dress terribly too.

There are times, however, when it's okay to tell him about appropriate attire for a certain occasion. For example, you can say, "My company's holiday party is formal dress," so that he won't show up in baggy jeans and an "I'm with Stupid" T-shirt—just like he'd have the right to tell you not to wear clear plastic stripper heels to his company party. Matters of appropriateness are fine to address directly—matters of taste are not.

Lazy Girl Hack: Help Him Out

A smarter approach to your man's woeful wardrobe is to gently and subtly make improvements. According to a Los Angeles–based personal shopper, a lot of guys are the types who have literally been waiting around for a woman like you to come along and dress them. These "malleable" types are very open to fashion transformations by your stylish self. Still, though, you don't want to come out and *say* that you're making him over. Instead, take an awful item—a T-shirt, for example—and find a more stylish upgrade for him. Meanwhile, you can "lose" the old item in the bottom of the laundry hamper. Just about every type of clothing has a more stylish equivalent—except Christmas sweaters. (If your guy has those, you might just have to get him to convert to a new religion.)

Lazy Girl Hack: Reward Improvements

If the only reason you're not trying to change your guy's wardrobe is because you don't want a confrontation, try using positive reinforcement. When he looks especially suave and fashionable, tell him how handsome he looks. Shower him with praise. Go wild with affection—whatever it takes to get him to make the correlation that "good outfit equals happy." And in fact, you probably will naturally be even more attracted to him if he's dressed like your favorite male model. So rather than insulting his iffy fashion choices, overwhelm him with love when he dresses well. Before you know it, you'll have him looking good enough to send out for an occasional trip to the grocery store!

PROBLEM

Your Boyfriend Isn't Funny, but Is Super Sensitive

Aside from prancing around in sexy lingerie and cooking delicious food, what's the top advice you see for women on how to win the heart of a guy? If you guessed *laugh at his jokes*, you win. Your prize? Lots of really stupid jokes to laugh at. Enjoy!

The male ego, from what we've learned about it thus far, seems to be wrapped up in a few things: sexual prowess, success at work, and a sense of humor. For whatever reason, being funny is an important part of being a man. Yet trying to laugh at a totally unfunny joke is like being told to feel amazingly wonderful when your hand touches a hot stove. It's just not natural. And some of the worst fake laughs I've ever heard have been those polite, sickly sweet, overdone laughs of women (my own included). What does a man's fake laugh even sound like? Does anyone even know? Probably not, because laughter isn't one of the things guys fake. They're more worried about pretending they're going to call you, or faking not having a thing for your best friend. Yay! Now there's a joke to laugh at!

But you love your guy—just not his jokes—and if you have to fake a laugh every so often to keep the peace, these hacks will make it easy for you.

Lazy Girl Hack: Put Your Hand over Your Mouth

It's true. Clamping a hand over your mouth while pretending to laugh will increase the believability of your fake laugh. Not sure why, except that maybe covering your mouth hides the fact that you're actually scowling? Probably, too, the hand-over-the-mouth trick muffles some of the phony, high-pitched abrasiveness of the fake-girl laugh. Also, if you are about to vomit over the stupidity of his joke, covering your mouth might conceal that to some degree as well. So, the hand-over-the-mouth method can serve as a catchall. Literally.

Lazy Girl Hack: Laugh at Your Own Jokes Too

If you use your fake laugh to punctuate your own jokes, too, then your guy will be more likely to believe it is real. Of course, he'll then think of you as a person who laughs at your own jokes, but hey, *someone* ought to laugh at them! You're a funny girl!

The idea is, if you use the same laugh for your own jokes that you use for his, it has to be legit. It's sort of like the notion that if you serve yourself coffee from the same pot that you serve his from, it's less likely that there's arsenic in it. Be careful, though—sometimes your jokes are quite good, and you might catch yourself unleashing a genuine guffaw or two for yourself. He'll recognize the contrast between real and fake right away.

Lazy Girl Hack: Get a Laugh Track

Remember those laugh tracks from old sitcoms? They were cues that people were supposed to laugh—which, when you think about it, must mean the jokes were pretty lame. What you can do is get him a laugh track, which he can activate when he's told a joke, or just when he wants to enter the room in a funny way like Lenny and Squiggy on *Laverne & Shirley*. When he pushes the laugh button, you will know that it is time for you to also laugh. If you don't quite hit the mark, all of those other people laughing will make him feel a ton better. And maybe, if it's needed, you can get a live studio audience "applause track" for his, ahem, intimate performances. He'll feel like he's been inducted into the Bedroom Hall of Fame! Just be careful you don't hit the laugh button by mistake.

PROBLEM

Your Boyfriend Wants to Netflix and Chill, but You're Not Feeling It

Ah, guys! Once we've weeded out the ones whose personalities force us to fake being awake, we find a good one, make a commitment, and begin a life of pretending to be asleep. Talk about irony, right?

In a perfect world, the old sleep fake isn't something you should need to do very often. However, you don't live in a perfect world—you live in a world where your boss's tantrums are eerily similar to your three-year-old nephew's (although hopefully your nephew's tantrums don't culminate in an epic grain-alcohol bender), your mother-in-law has insisted on making you bedazzled pajamas that say "Married to a Mama's Boy," and your to-do list might be longer than the Bible. All of this leaves you with a total lack of a sex drive, but then here comes your man, asking if you want to Netflix and chill. Netflix? Always. It's the chill part you're not feeling tonight. Quick, put on those bedazzled PJs, close your eyes, and try out some of these hacks for the laziest of lazy girl fakes.

Lazy Girl Hack: Don't Snore!

One of the fastest ways to expose yourself for the lame sleep faker you are is to attempt to fake snore. Fake snoring usually only works if: (a) your partner is heartbreakingly gullible; (b) you are amazingly convincing; or (c) you are both *Looney Tunes* characters. If none of these apply to you, it's best not to even try for the snore. Most people can't help but exaggerate their fake snores, giving them a theatrical, over-the-top chainsaw quality most often seen in horror flicks or mass deforestation. It's especially unconvincing if you don't even snore in the first place! So skip the snore—there's no point in making life harder than it already is. Just mouth-breathe deeply (more on this later) and count opossums—that's the animal you should count to summon pretend sleep. Yeah, I just made that up.

You Know You're a Lazy Girl When . . .
You actually fall asleep when you pretend to be asleep to avoid sex. Hey, you might as well get some use of the vertical downtime.

Lazy Girl Hack: Drool in the Dark

Okay, so it's definitely gross, but most people do drool while they're asleep. This is because during sleep, we tend to breathe through our mouths, and we have less control over our facial muscles in general. So to add a little extra authenticity, you might want to drool just a bit while faking sleep. This is not too difficult to do; just breathe through your mouth and it should happen naturally. Or think of a shirtless Hugh Jackman. Do *not* spit—not unless you're very sure of your aim. Otherwise, what was meant to be a gentle sparing of his feelings could end up being the most insulting "no, thanks" he's ever received. (Note: Drooling can potentially backfire if your guy thinks you are drooling over him. Use this approach carefully.)

Ideally, though, your drool won't be too much of an issue, because you will be doing your fakery in the inky void of total darkness. After all, everything is easier to fake in the dark . . .

Lazy Girl Hack: Sleepwalk

It is possible that despite your efforts to seem asleep, your guy is just so crazy about you that he's going to keep trying no matter what. In this case, you can try to evade him by sleepwalking. Get out of bed, making sure to keep your eyes open, but stare blankly like a zombie. Grunt or babble incoherently as you plod around the house. Do this until he gives up and falls asleep (listen for the snore!). If he follows you, you can try sleep running, but I'm not sure that's a real thing. Definitely, sleep-getting-into-your-car-and-driving-to-a-hotel-so-you-can-get-some-peace is not an actual thing, so don't expect him to buy that.

PROBLEM

You Hate Your Partner's Friends, but Like Him Too Much to Say Anything

You love your man, but oh, good God almighty—his *friends*. They are the type who test out electronic dog collars on themselves for fun, Photoshop your head onto the Playmate of the Month's body, and haven't read a book since high school English class.

Basically, your man's only friends who aren't half-bald, paunchy, thirty-something kindergarteners are his *ex-girlfriends*. And while Ashley, Jenn, and Krista are much less likely to show up at your house and pull each other's fingers, they're more likely to give you backhanded compliments ("I think you look *fabulous* with that extra weight") while reminiscing about the "good old days" with your guy. It's a good thing their skinny little shoulders are way too sharp for him to cry on comfortably, because every time you get in a fight, the Bony Bitch Brigade is right there, offering him its puny consolation.

If it were up to you, you'd lose all of this deadwood and pick out some nice new friends for your guy. But it isn't up to you. What to do?

Lazy Girl Hack: Give Him Lots of Space

One way to convincingly like being able to stand your guy's friends is to encourage him to spend lots of "alone time" with them. Tell him you understand that he needs time with his friends—so do you. So offer the occasional "friend night," where he goes out with his buddies and you and your girlfriends get all dolled up and go out for a night on the town. Maybe one of your friends will want to post pictures on social media of the bunch of you looking gorgeous and having fun on your own. These pictures will, no doubt, be followed by "likes" or comments like "Hot mamas!" from assorted males, perhaps even your partner's knuckle-dragging friends. Note: You *cannot* take this too far; don't go around acting flirty with other guys. Just remind him that you are totally not threatened by his friends and have an exciting, thumbs-up-worthy life of your own. This will make him want to take a night off from the cavemen and put some effort into deserving the prize he's won.

Lazy Girl Hack: Win Over the Exes

If your man is still friendly with his exes, the very worst thing you can do is act threatened by them. Being upset by their continued presence in his life shows that you are insecure and might seem like a lack of trust. Even if you don't trust them, you need to be able to trust him, or else, what's the point?

You need to not only accept them, but embrace them. No, I don't mean make out with them during the football halftime show—I mean become friends with them. This might be difficult at first, but keep at it. What you need to do is treat them like any other friend of his, except better, because they're women and you can connect over girl stuff. Compliment a new hairstyle or outfit. Say, "I really love the thin swath of material that you identify as a dress," or "That's a really cute 'I Still Love My Ex' T-shirt." Eventually, they will warm up to you and see that you really don't view them as rivals—because you know they're never going to get him back. And if they get sad, tell them you have a perfectly soft, well-nourished shoulder for them to cry on. Aw!

PROBLEM

You Don't Get Along with Your Boyfriend's Family, but Can Never Tell Him

You've been dating your guy for about six months now, and you know he's The One. You've gotten through the first-date awkwardness, the conceal-your-insecurities phase, and the okay-you-can-see-me-without-makeup phase, and he has passed each test with flying colors. Even better, he is totally in love with you too. He even thinks it's adorable when you have PMS and cry into your Heath Bar Crunch ice cream that you're eating out of the container and dripping all over your can't-wear-out-of-the-house leggings. You know, almost without a doubt, that you are going to stay with this man for the rest of your life. After meeting his family, though, you're starting to hope that the rest of your life will be mercifully short.

Seriously, this family is truly a can of mixed nuts. His mom is an overbearing oedipal nightmare who calls your boyfriend "my little man" and "accidentally" wanders into your bedroom when visiting due to her "poor night vision." His dad is an obsessively materialistic financial something-or-other who stops insulting your boyfriend's English degree only long enough to swill another whiskey and wink creepily. His sister believes fervently that she and her "saved" friends will be raptured to heaven in the end, and that your boyfriend is now damned to hell because you are a "heathen." These people are pretty much the exact combination of everything that annoys you, under one roof. Yet this guy is the guy you want to make your future home with and you don't want to cause conflict with your future in-laws. Don't worry, lazy girl! These hacks will help you hide your true feelings about your bae's mom and dad till death do you part.

Lazy Girl Hack: What Doesn't Kill You . . .

The truth is, families are people we randomly are forced to spend our lives with through genetic accident. Sometimes we come to love them because we want to, but mostly, we love them because we have to. You didn't choose these people, but neither did your boyfriend. And what didn't kill him obviously made him stronger.

Just think—his mom's clinginess and lack of boundaries led him to be a strong, independent person who always knocks before he enters a room. His dad's alcoholic greed-mongering led him to be a principled, generous guy who drinks moderately and winks only when his contact lenses are irritated. And his sister's fire-and-brimstone routine has helped him develop logic, religious tolerance, and a prosperous End of Days pet-sitting service.

You might not relate to these people, but they've unintentionally helped shape this guy into the man you love. Remember that, and thank them for it.

Lazy Girl Hack: Pretend It's Opposite Day

One great rule of thumb for how to talk about his family is to take whatever you actually think, run it through a special "family filter" in your head, and let it come out as something nice. So instead of saying "Your mom is bizarrely obsessed with you and thinks you're her husband," say, "I love the way your mom adores you and enjoys your company." Instead of saying, "Your dad is an alcoholic, soulless materialist," say, "Your dad clearly enjoys his career success." Just always say the opposite of what you think, or a positive-sounding version of the horrible thing you think. And unless they do something horrible to you, do not speak your true thoughts to your man. This will not help your cause at all. Talk to your girlfriends, to your sister—anyone but him.

Lazy Girl Hack: If You Can't Beat 'em, Join 'em

In the beginning, getting used to another family's dysfunction is a bit of a shock. You've had your whole life to absorb and become accustomed to your own weird family. Remember, you didn't choose your folks, so why worry about whether these are the in-laws you would have chosen? You chose him, and that's the choice that matters. And just think, eventually—maybe over a lifetime—you will become so used to them that you love them like your own family. Which is to say, you find them annoying, frustrating, and difficult, but they've wormed their way into your heart anyway.

If nothing else, think about the family you want to start with him someday (although, at six months, that is *not* cool to talk about!). That's a family you will choose. And oh, boy, when Grandma and Grandpa come to visit . . .

PROBLEM

You Couldn't Care Less about Sports, but Your Boyfriend's a Fanatic

It's that season again—let's just call it *boyfriend season*—when you are called upon to pretend you enjoy watching sports and participating in "jock culture" or face being a sports widow for months on end.

Whether it's football, baseball, basketball, or that sport with the flying broomsticks they play in Harry Potter (actually, if your man is into this, you might not have to worry about jock culture), your man's obsession with his sport of choice probably rivals his obsession with you. Which, really, is kind of annoying—the only brawny men in tight pants who should ever be a threat to you are the rogue pirates in your swashbuckling hijack fantasy.

Nevertheless, the fine tradition of men and sports probably dates all the way back to the Roman Empire, when wives were rumored to have complained, "Oh, you and your gladiator games with your precious buddies. God forbid I should ask you to stay home and watch little Ovid while *my* friends and I go get our fortunes read through bird guts."

Do you want to be that complaining harpy? No. Rather than competing with the sport, you want to embrace it so your man will embrace you. Once you win him over for keeps, you can drop this whole façade and go back to watching HGTV. But for now, you need to take the lazy path of least resistance and pretend to be a fan.

Lazy Girl Hack: Dress the Part

As a female, you'll find that one potentially enjoyable part of being a faux sports fan is to assemble your sporty wardrobe. For this I recommend a casual but deliberate look—tight, low-rise jeans that, from a barstool perspective, reveal your temporary lower-back tattoo of his team.

Also, a jersey for his team is a great idea. Don't worry about having to wear some hideous color—they make jerseys for all teams in pink these days, just for us girly fans. They also make fitted little baby tees and ringer tees for women whose interest in sports is aimed mostly at scoring that man.

When choosing a jersey, you also have to decide which player you want represented on your back. This is easy—just pick the hottest guy on the team who is also skilled at football. This will not only show that you're an awesome sport, but will no doubt make your man jealous. Well done!

Lazy Girl Hack: Join a Fantasy League

As ridiculous as it may sound, you can also worm your way into his sports-loving heart by participating in fantasy league play. By doing this, you can learn some important sports terms, endear yourself to his friends with good-natured trash talking, and really lock in his affections. You guys could even play a secret little "fantasy" game, where every time a player on his fantasy team scores, *he* scores. This will create a Pavlovian association between sports and your sexy self, allowing you to infiltrate (and maybe even replace) sports in his mind. Touchdown!

Honestly, though, joining a fantasy league will at least force you to know some of the players and have someone to root for when you're stuck watching for hours on end. And there are fantasy leagues for everything out there. Fantasy baseball? Check! Fantasy football? Check? Fantasy college basketball? Yup, even that. Just a note: You only really set your lineups for fantasy football once a week, so this may be the option for you, lazy girl!

Lazy Girl Hack: Let the Other Ladies Know

Okay, so you've transformed yourself into a jersey-wearing, fantasy sports–playing chick. That's great, but you should be prepared to get some dirty looks from your fellow women. For many of us, a sports-loving woman is a traitor to our gender. So expect appalled stares from the wives of your man's friends as you jock it up with the guys over Buffalo wings. They'll roll their eyes and saunter away in their nonsporty stilettos, leaving you with three belching men and a fourth guy's name on your back.

"Wait!" you want to scream. "This isn't really me! I'm just doing this to lock in that guy! Come *back*!"

This type of confusion is exactly why I think there should be some international signal for sports fakery between women. Here's what I propose—a cheap replica of a Super Bowl ring, worn on the engagement ring finger. This will symbolize that sports are merely a strategy, a placeholder for the lifetime commitment you seek. Once you get that other ring, this Super Bowl ring will come off like a prom dress. Or, more specifically, like a wedding dress.

PROBLEM

You Hate the Outdoors, but Your Boyfriend Is a Mountain Man

So, you've landed yourself an outdoorsy type. Good for you! Often, outdoorsy guys are resourceful, rugged, and generally in awesome physical shape (unless by "outdoorsy" you mean "homeless"). He seems really cool and interesting, and he appears to be into you, as well. Now, he's trying to take things to the next level—he's invited you on a camping trip! It will be a beautiful weekend of communing with nature and getting back to the basics of life. He's basically beckoned you into his inner sanctum.

The problem? There are few things that sound less attractive to you than sleeping on the ground, being in such close proximity to snakes, bugs, and snake and bug poop, and not being able to scroll through social media because there isn't any cell reception in what's basically the middle of nowhere. Basically, you are about as hearty as a piece of tissue paper in a tsunami, and you much prefer *campy* to *camping*. The last time a guy told you he was "pitching a tent," he was talking dirty, and your idea of "roughing it" is waking up without a Grande Cinnamon Dolce Frappuccino . . . or at least a dependable K-Cup.

But go along with it just this once—you might win him over forever. Hopefully, on future trips, he'll opt for guys' weekends with his best pal, since you'll have proven yourself. But just because you're camping doesn't mean you have to go all out. Here are some hacks to help you through.

Lazy Girl Hack: Gear Up

As I've mentioned, the best way for a girl to get excited about any hobby is to accessorize. You're lucky, in that camping happens to be a hobby with a full wardrobe attached to it. Imagine if your guy was into backgammon or something!

This will be fun—an excuse to buy a bunch of stuff. Go to your nearest camping or sporting goods store (or just scroll through their inventory on your phone while you enjoy things like electricity and running water), and stock up on hiking boots, a parka, socks, a sleeping bag, vests, and a cute backpack.

At least you'll feel good about what you're wearing and sleeping in . . . even if you hate everything else about the trip.

You Know You're a Lazy Girl When . . .

You take the fact that you're camping as an excuse to put your hair in braids for the whole weekend and never take it down. One less thing to worry about.

Lazy Girl Hack: Light His Fire

If you want to really impress this guy, you can offer to start a campfire for him. There are a few quick and easy cheats for achieving this. Duraflame and other firelog companies sell outdoor crackling logs, which you can combine with some real tinder to create a fast fire. It's recommend that you put the crackling log on the bottom, light it on both ends, and place the real logs on top of it.

You Know You're a Lazy Girl When . . .

Your only experience with tinder is swiping right.

Other camping supply companies sell parabolic mirrors to start a quick fire. For this to work, you have to have full sunlight so that the mirror can reflect the sun to create fire. Follow the directions that come with the product and make sure the mirror you buy is designed for camping. You don't want to just be staring at your own pretty face all night—although that's a great way to make sure your makeup is right. Once you have that fire lit, the two of you can cozy up in your sleeping bags—or better yet, in the same sleeping bag!

PROBLEM

You're Chilling with Your Guy after a Date and Nature Calls

You have met an amazing guy, quite possibly the Love of Your Life, and you've been spending practically all of your waking hours together. It's a beautiful nonstop montage of long kisses, whispered plans of your future in the middle of the night, cuddling, and romantic dinners out on the town. He treats you like a delicate, beautiful flower, and he stares at you with wonder that such a rare, magical creature as you could exist. No one has ever made you feel so beautiful, and so feminine.

So it would be really bad, after one of those romantic dinners at your favorite Mexican restaurant, for you to dump the foul contents of your intestines in his bathroom. Very un-flowerlike, even if you open a window and light a match.

The sad fact is, in the beginning of a relationship, guys in love tend to put a woman on a ridiculous, exalted pedestal, and this pedestal does *not* happen to include a toilet. Guys don't like to think women sweat, or belch, or use the lower halves of their bodies for anything but monogamous sex with them.

Maybe you've found an extraordinarily amazing guy who doesn't care one bit about whether you create unpleasant aromas in his bathroom. But you don't want to find out if he feels that way. Fortunately, you can get through this . . . but you might want to put a halt to all the Mexican food.

Lazy Girl Hack: Use Public Restrooms

One excellent trick is to make frequent use of public restrooms during this pedestal phase of your relationship. When you're out on dates—which you frequently will be because he's trying to win you over—slip away into the restroom to take care of your business. One great advantage for us women is that in most cases, it doesn't take as long for us to perform this task as it does for guys. Get it done and over with quickly and shamelessly. Because you're using a ladies' restroom, there will be no chance of him catching you. Sadly, this means inflicting your nasty business on other women, which is all too often a casualty of dating. Just offer a sheepish expression and a shrug to any woman you see, and she will understand. She's probably there doing the same thing.

Lazy Girl Hack: Potty Train Your Cat

This one will possibly take some time to achieve, but in return, it'll provide you with years and years of bathroom subterfuge. If you have a cat—and you know you do—you can teach your cat to use the toilet. There are tons of purchasable training methods that enable you to teach your cat to effectively use the bathroom receptacles. And if your man is staying with you in your house, you can *blame your cat* for the smell in the bathroom. Simply say, "Oh, Mittens, boy did you ever make a doozy this time!" shortly after you've exited the bathroom. This strategy has the distinct advantage that you can continue to use it after the two of you move in together or get married. Just make sure Mittens comes with you. Remember, though, cats don't live forever—so you might want to work on having kids as soon as possible. Then you can blame them!

Lazy Girl Hack: Wait a Long Time

If you are in a situation where you are forced to use a shared bathroom where your man could walk in, you should wait as long as it takes for the smell to clear the air. You might be waiting a while. While your waiting, just say that you have to take a shower. I advise going to the bathroom first, then taking the shower. It's possible that the time, combined with the smell of shampoo and soap, will help reverse your odor.

Lazy Girl Hack: Be Proactive

If engaging in a "waiting game" challenge with your own waste isn't your idea of time well spent, there are also Poo-Pourri products out there with charming names like Potty Potion and Trap-A-Crap that claim to stop bathroom odors before they even start. Just spritz them into the commode *before* you do the deuce. The secret apparently lies in the essential oils, which create a "barrier" on the water's surface to prevent odors from escaping. Poo-Pourri products are packaged in an assortment of delightful fragrances, including grapefruit, lemongrass, and blood orange.

PROBLEM

You Have a Sordid Past and Your New Guy Is Mr. Perfect

So, it's gotten to that point in your relationship known as the "confessional stage." You've declared love for one another, and you spend your magical days gazing into each other's eyes, marveling at how lucky you are to have found each other. In fact, you two are so in love, it's hard to even imagine the other having a life (and loves!) before you.

"So, what about the guys before me?" he asks dreamily. "Tell me all about it. I want to know everything about you."

Uh-oh. This is a tough one. Guys claim they want to know all about your sexual past, but really, they only want to know stuff that will make them feel better (we're the same way, by the way). You want to be entirely honest, since you're pouring your hearts out to one another, but you suspect there are a few things in your past that would be best kept under wraps. How do you spin your history without sounding shady and secretive, *or* without overdoing it?

Lazy Girl Hack: Men Need to Win

Here is a crucial piece of male psychology that should guide you in faking your sexual history: When it comes to sex, *men need to win*. According to GoodMenProject.com, the reason guys get so freaked out when a woman has had a lot of sexual partners is because that means more competition. If he's only competing against five people, he's more likely to rank number one than if he's competing with fifty. For reasons that are not entirely known but might have something to do with all those competing sperm for that one egg, sex is a game guys need to win.

So when fabricating your sexual past, remember that your current guy needs to be Number One. That's why, in general, I think it's more to your benefit to play your number down rather than play it up. Either way, though, you will need to convince him, like Mirror, Mirror on the Wall, that he is the most potent, long-lasting and pleasure-giving of them all. If you even so much as insinuate that another guy outperformed him, you will never, ever be allowed to forget about this, for the rest of your life.

Lazy Girl Hack: Skip the Details

For the reasons described previously, you should avoid going into detail about your sexual past, unless they happen to be details that make your previous lovers seem like incompetent oafs. You can tell a funny story about the guy who wore a prosthetic penis in his pants, or the guy who thought you would like it if he slathered you in Thousand Island salad dressing. But details about stuff that you actually enjoyed should be kept mum. Even if your guy says he's trying to find out what you like, that's not the route to go in telling him. Guys are fairly persistent about this, so be on guard. He might say something like, "Come on, there must have been some guy who knew how to give you what you wanted." Just smile mysteriously and say, "Not like you do," and give him a big kiss. He's the big winner!

You Know You're a Lazy Girl When . . .

Your dream guy is someone who is "woke" and your nightmare guy is someone who woke you up.

Lazy Girl Hack: Careful with the Experiments

Guys might also press to find out about other crazy things you've done, such as experimentation with other girls or threesomes. Unless he seems like a very open-minded guy, refrain from discussing any such thing. However, some guys genuinely do enjoy the idea of their woman being a little bit kinky, particularly when it comes to bi-curious adventures. If you think your man is this kind of guy, feel free to give him information in small doses and see how he takes it. The point you want to get across to him is that even if he's not your first, you want him to be your last. Winner takes all!

PROBLEM

Your Partner Only Eats Healthy Food, but You're a Total Snacker

You're dating a new guy you really like and have reached the crucial stage of trying to figure out what's wrong with him. Is this guy secretly a neo-Nazi, is he the head of a large polygamous family, or does he enjoy dressing up in women's clothing? You've been nervously waiting for the other shoe to drop, and hoping it is not a Jimmy Choo strappy sandal in size fourteen wide.

Finally, you discover his fatal flaw, and it turns out that this flaw is actually a "good" thing—the guy is an obsessive health food junkie.

This might be good for most people, but for you, who usually has cheese curl dust on your fingers and considers "corn syrup" to be a food group, this is some seriously bad news. All your life, you've had a taste for nutritionally empty food items—the saltier, fattier, and more synthetic, the better. You adore sugary soft drinks, butter-loaded popcorn, and artery-clogging bacon, preferably chocolate-covered. You attend state fairs just for the deep-fried Oreos. And through some thoroughly unfair stroke of genetic luck, you have managed to get away with your horrific diet. You've had no complaints. Then one day, Mr. New Guy offers to cook for you at his house—a sweet gesture and a good sign for the relationship. Except he serves you lightly sautéed vegetables and brown rice. You're all for eating healthy, but veggies and rice are not going to cut it when you have a snack stash hidden away in your coffee table drawers at home. All is not lost, though. You can still make this work—for a while anyway.

Lazy Girl Hack: Keep a Stash at Work

Okay, so you obviously are not going to be able to enjoy your favorite greasy, sugary delights at your man's house. Although you could keep a nasty little stash of Funyuns, cookie dough cupcakes, and candy bars at your own house, it is possible that he may also want to visit your home, right? And you want him to! So, unfortunately, your only "neutral zone" is going to be at work, where you will want to store an extensive junk food stash in your desk. This may cause your coworkers to suspect that you are pregnant, but that's not your problem right now. Your problem is being able to hold on to that gorgeous man while still being able to pump your arteries full of Cheez Whiz, MSG, and sugar on a daily basis. If you gorge on fatty, horrible food all day at work, it will not only enable you to go to his house for an angelic dinner of organic couscous salad, but it will make your job that much more enjoyable. If, by some chance, you also work with this guy, though, you're screwed. You are either going to have to break up with him or start eating healthy food. The choice is yours, but—you know—men come and go, but Nacho Cheese Pretzel Combos are forever.

You Know You're a Lazy Girl When . . .
Becoming "hangry" is about as energetic as you get.

Lazy Girl Hack: The Timing Is Great

Listen here, lazy girl—you might be getting away with dietary murder now, but you're not getting any younger. The fact is, the older you get, the more your hyperactive little metabolism will slow down, and the more your body will be vulnerable to various types of breakdown. If you continue to treat yourself so horribly (even though deep-fried Reese's Peanut Butter Cups feel like the best treatment ever), your body is going to punish you. That's almost a guarantee.

Luckily for you, the timing on your little ruse is just perfect. In the early stages of your relationship, you can go ahead and pig out in secret while you act all kale-loving to his face (if you get caught, claim you have a side job as a professional eater).

But by the time things get serious enough to lead to cohabitation or marriage, you will probably be reaching an age where it's smart to drop foods that spell "cheese" with a "z" anyway. So, yes, I'm telling you to fake it for a while, but then *actually improve your diet*. You are lucky—this guy came along and is going to not only steal your heart, but rescue its various valves and arteries. He's practically a giant defibrillator—keep him around, if only as your personal chef!

PART 4

Half-Ass-ing It at Home

There's something about housework that's pretty close to horrible. You're at the place where your bed, your snacks, and your comfy pants are, but you're forced to push them away and spend your time scrubbing the toilet, entertaining company, or making the kitchen you just half-assed cleaned dirty again by cooking dinner for your friends? This is where you need to take a stand, lazy girl! Even though you do (at least sometimes) have to say yes to cleaning out your car or making sure your parents don't judge your apartment, you don't have to spend as much energy on it as you might think—thanks to these lazy girl hacks.

PROBLEM

You're Out of Clean Clothes, but Need to Leave the House

Okay, you've been so busy and stressed this week you've barely had time to inhale necessary and lifesaving air, let alone do laundry. And laundry is just such a time-suck. You not only have to separate your darks and lights, get it in the machine, and swap the load in the dryer, you have to actually fold the clothes and then put them away in your drawers. At least that's how this is supposed to work. But let's be honest, you've been living out of laundry bins (or even your dryer) for weeks now and you've noticed that your dirty bins are starting to overtake the ones you're using as a bureau.

Then it happens. You absolutely have to leave the house for the day and there's a chance you're going to see people you know. Dirty sweatshirts and those stinky leggings with the holes in the crotch aren't going to cut it. You have to use some clean clothes hacks, and fast!

Lazy Girl Hack: Buy New Clothes

If you happen to have a fair amount of disposable income, you can have "disposable clothes." Not really disposable—you don't want to actually throw your dirty clothes out—but you can use them as a great excuse to go shopping for some new clothes! Just put the icky stuff in the hamper and hit the stores, where you can outfit yourself in brand-new, clean items in the blink of an eye. If you happen to be one of those people who feel the need to wash brand-new clothes before you wear them, I'm sorry to report that you're doomed either way. I would also point out that if you have time to go shopping, you probably have time to wash clothes. Sorry, just saying.

You Know You're a Lazy Girl When . . .
You get so irritated when your bra straps get all twisted up with other laundry, you usually give up and retire every item involved in the tangle.

Lazy Girl Hack: Spray Them Down

For any clothes that don't have visible stains or don't smell horrendous, you have the option of spraying them with air freshener and letting them tumble in the dryer for a while. However, clothes with difficult or stubborn stains (ahem . . . red wine) or those that might be the victims of heavy perspiration (men's clothes) might not be good options for this hack. There's only so much that air freshener can do.

Lazy Girl Hack: Use a Wash and Fold Service

Theoretically, you could take your clothes to the laundromat, but who has time to sit around trying to find coins and waiting for your clothes to be done? If you had that kind of time, you'd wash them yourself.

Fortunately, quite a few laundromats also offer a "wash and fold" service, where you can get a load of laundry washed, dried, *and* folded by the laundromat employees. Most of these services charge by the pound of laundry. The beauty is that you can drop off your nasty clothes and have them washed, dried, and folded while you do other necessary stuff. The laundromat does not, however, put your clothes away in your drawers, so you at least have that to put off doing.

You Know You're a Lazy Girl When . . .

You regularly do a smell test to see if you can wear something again without washing it.

PROBLEM

Your Car's a Mess, but You're the Driver for the Night

You're heading out for a night with your friends and it's your turn to drive. You don't mind. There's something fun about being behind the wheel when you're heading out for a night with your besties. Unfortunately, even though you don't mind, you clearly didn't think this through because your car is a total disaster.

There are month-old snacks that now look like dehydrated tongues, assorted receipts that probably contain itemized humiliation (extra-absorbency tampons, $5.95; Save-A-Lot brand stool softener, $4.50; Bunion Care Gel Sleeve, $11.95; Doritos, $4.95), and a veritable sea of empty coffee cups scattered all over the interior. This is not even to mention the broken sunglasses, dog hair, and random small change wedged between the seats.

You need to get your ride up to par quick! You're picking up your friends in about an hour, so let the hacking begin!

Lazy Girl Hack: Hide the Clutter

Your first step in reducing your car's chances of appearing on *Hoarders: Car Edition* is to remove all the junk and clutter. Simply grab one trash bag and one box for storage. Everything that is trash (which will probably be most of what you find) goes right into the bag, and everything else goes into the box. You can store the box in your garage, or even in the trunk like some shameful corpse you're hiding. If you don't feel as though you have time to make these life-altering decisions about trash vs. nontrash, you can just put everything in the box for now. But seriously, if you do this maybe you really are a car hoarder.

Lazy Girl Hack: Make a Blanket Statement

You probably don't have time for a full car vacuum, or to go to a car wash to have the interior vacuumed for you. If you do have time for either of these, go for it! If not, don't worry: You can implement a quick fix.

Simply drape blankets on the seats to cover up any stains, hairs, or other funky items that might not be easily removable. Your passengers might wonder why there are blankets on the seats, but they also probably won't *really* want to know. So respect the part of them that doesn't want to know and don't tell them. If they start annoying you with questions, tell them you use the blankets to conceal the bodies of your victims prior to dumping them in the ocean. That'll bring the conversation (and probably the carpool) to a halt.

If the whole blanket scenario seems a bit too rustic for you, plenty of companies sell seat covers, for the very purpose of covering stains *and* protecting your car from future messes. Plus, everyone knows how hard it is to wrap a body in a car seat cover!

Lazy Girl Hack: Add Some New-Car Smell

The final step for making your car acceptable for carpool day is to freshen up that smell. There are now a ton of different types of air fresheners available for cars—you don't have to have a whole forest of those little trees anymore. There are sprays, gels, plug-ins, "fragrance cartridges," cans, and vent clips. You can get your car to smell like everything from candy to fresh laundry. Although why would you be doing laundry in your car? Do you, like, live in there or something?

PROBLEM

You Were Supposed to Cook Dinner, but Were Too Busy

It has been one of those annoying "hurry up and wait" days—those frustrating combinations of panic and drudgery that leave you unsure whether to reach for your antidepressants or your anxiety meds. First, you rush into work just to sit in a conference room, waiting for your boss to show up for an early meeting. Then you hurry back to your desk to call a client for a scheduled phone call, and wait on hold, listening to Rod Stewart ballads (yes, he *has* told you lately that he loves you, the last time this stupid song came on). At lunchtime, you hurry to the DMV to renew your license, and wait in a long line of annoyed people to have a terribly unflattering picture taken.

As if that wasn't bad enough, tonight you're entertaining a few people for dinner, so you hurry to your car, wait in traffic, hurry home and wait for your glacier-slow oven to preheat. You have a delicious recipe you plan to make—roasted chicken with rosemary potatoes. Then you take a closer look and realize that instead of needing to cook for twenty minutes, this dish needs to cook for 200 minutes! Oh, and you forgot to even take the bird out of the freezer to defrost. Unfortunately, your guests are coming in an hour, so "hurry up and wait" isn't going to cut it. Just "hurry up!"

Lazy Girl Hack: Hit the Grocery Deli

The deli department of your local grocery store is the best friend you can have when faking a home-cooked meal—unless your dinner guests are such awesome friends that you can tell them this whole ridiculous story, and they will just laugh and give you lots of big hugs (but for now, just stick with that deli).

Most grocery stores provide a wide array of freshly made meat and side dishes, such as roasted chicken, fish, or beef. And many will even broil up some salmon or chicken for you on the spot. How cool is that? Literally, someone is cooking your dinner for you. So pick something delicious and maybe even healthy, and grab some side dishes while you're at it. While you're waiting for your salmon to broil, pick up a loaf of good bread and a bagged salad. Just throw in some plum or cherry tomatoes, some dressing, and maybe some croutons, cheese, or other flourishes. Your friends will be amazed at what a good cook you are!

You Know You're a Lazy Girl When . . .

Your two favorite kitchen appliances are the microwave and the Crock-Pot because you like to switch it up between "quick and lazy" and "slow and lazy."

Lazy Girl Hack: Add Your Personal Touch

The next step, once you get the food home, is to remove any and all signs of store-boughtness, including packaging, labels, nutrition information, and "Day Old/Half Off Sale" stickers. You must undo all their efforts to make the food look professionally made. So pull out your personal serving platters, serving spoons, and dishes. And serving these foods with items from your own pantry (steak sauce, salad dressing, salt and pepper, etc.) will definitely add to the illusion of a home-cooked meal. Then, just open a bottle of wine or two, and voilà! Hurry up and wait for the compliments to come pouring in!

PROBLEM

You're Supposed to Bake Something for a Fundraiser, but You Can't Get It Done in Time

Your friend is an amazing person and is putting together a fundraiser for something or someone she really cares about. That's the good thing. The bad thing is that she's pretty much forcing you to bring a homemade item for the bake sale she's having as part of the event and you don't have the time or energy for this. You work a crazy full-time job and you value your downtime. And you really don't even know how to bake. Here are some bakery hacks to save the day—and your friendship with this person who clearly thinks you have more free time (or an inclination to help others) than you actually do.

Lazy Girl Hack: Buy the Cookies

Go buy some damn cookies! However, if you're going to pass them off as homemade, you need to deliberately create imperfections in your bakery-bought confections. Jessie Oleson Moore, of www.cakespy.com, says that cookies, cupcakes, or cakes that look too perfect are a dead giveaway that you purchased them. So your job is to rough these baked goods up a bit so that everyone knows how you slaved over them.

For cookies, perfect symmetry of shape and a lack of overdone or browned bottoms might cause people to think "store-bought." So Oleson Moore advises the following fix: Put a pat of butter in a frying pan on medium heat, and while you wait for the butter to melt and bubble, use a knife to file gently away at the edges of your cookies. Then place them on the skillet and leave them on until they brown on the bottom. Then remove them, and use your hands to slightly dent the tops and sides to look "homemade." Tip: Don't completely mash or destroy them, or they will look like they were homemade by an insane baby. Another way to add a homemade touch is to add your own decorative flourishes to the cookies. You can use sprinkles, shredded coconut, glaze, or whatever you want—just keep it "real," a.k.a., random!

Lazy Girl Hack: Mess Up the Cupcakes

Oleson Moore rightly points out that the biggest problem with store-bought cupcakes is that ridiculously beautiful way they're decorated. That's fair enough; professional bakers and cake decorators take pride in their art. They want to show how much better they make a cupcake look than us mere amateurs. Sure, that's great, but you want these cupcakes to look like the creations of an amateur (an amateur *superwoman*, that is). So your job is to totally *undo* the decorator's beautiful work. They won't ever need to know!

Suppose, for example, that a professional pastry dispenser has doled out the icing on your cupcakes in those flawless little poufs. You need to flatten and level those gorgeous, sugary rosettes before they rat you out. Oleson Moore advises using a butter knife to gently spread the frosting out into more old-school, flawed coverage. Maybe even add some of your own sprinkles to make it look like something you're actually capable of making at home. Sure, it won't look as good, but that's the point. It will *taste* awesome, however.

P.S.: If anyone asks you for a recipe, Oleson Moore says you can noncommittally agree to email it, but never follow up. Hopefully, if you uglify your baked goods enough, no one will even realize their awesomeness until you're long gone!

PROBLEM

You're Bored Out of Your Mind on a Family Vacation

Oh, boy . . . Here you are, at your family reunion in Disney World! Lucky, lucky! In addition to being assaulted by sappy cartoonish schlock at every turn, being fondled by giant mice and ducks, and having that "It's a Small World" song echo through your brain like a mini-stroke, you get to see your long-lost extended family! Yay!

There they are, big as life, traipsing around happily in their mouse ears—aunts, uncles, cousins, nieces, nephews, and possibly a few inbred combinations of the above (it is a *very* small world, as it turns out). Oh, look, there's Goofy, with his two teeth and his oversize clown shoes—oh, wait, no, that's your cousin Raymond.

To say that this is not your dream vacation would be like saying that the sun is a little bit warm. You and your boyfriend have thrown away valuable vacation time in order to endure this cornucopia of awkwardness and forced jollity. If you had to break it down, this trip would be 95 percent obligation and 5 percent vacation, which is a total of *maybe* 6 percent actual fun.

The one thing that qualifies this as a vacation—the gorgeous weather—is beside the point, since it's June, and the weather is warm everywhere. You're going to need some serious "magic" to get you through this!

Lazy Girl Hack: Oblication: Accept It for What It Is

If your trip happens to be an obligation, the first step you can take is to come to terms with this. Yes, you can rail against the fact that you spent vacation time on this, but how will that help you? Instead of thinking of this as a vacation that's being destroyed by annoying family members, think of it as a family obligation that happens to include palm trees. Not to mention nice restaurants, potentially fun rides, and those extra-fluffy hotel pillows! If possible, try to find some small way to treat yourself: Order room service at the hotel, or escape with your bae to briefly visit the beach or have margaritas at an outdoor bar. And if you can't manage this, enjoy the people-watching for all it's worth. Just your family alone will provide days of intriguing case study.

Lazy Girl Hack: Remember, No Vacation Is Perfect

Think back to the many vacations you've had in your life. Some were better than others, certainly, but were any of them *perfect*? Doubtful. That's because we are humans, and humans are not perfect; therefore, human vacations cannot be perfect. Either your luggage got lost and didn't show up until the day you were leaving, or your boyfriend had that nasty sinus infection and you were stuck watching him irrigate his nose all week, or maybe you got sun poisoning on the first day and had to stay inside for the rest of the trip applying aloe.

Or maybe you just couldn't relax. Maybe you kept thinking of that project at work and whether your coworkers would do okay without you. Maybe you felt guilty about how much you ate and ended up spending half of your day in the gym working it off. Or maybe your boyfriend was the one preoccupied, and you were annoyed that he couldn't just be present in the moment. Do you see where I'm going? You might be able to unpack your bags on vacation, but you never really get to unload your baggage. So oftentimes, the same issues that haunted you back home come along for the trip.

This might sound very glass-half-empty, but it really isn't. It's about accepting the limitations of vacation, and therefore taking the pressure off yourself to "achieve" a great vacation. We're all nuts, and our vacations will always be a little bit messed up. It's okay. Hopefully, you can at least have a few pleasant memories. And you'll have your mouse ears to show for it.

PROBLEM

You Hate Your Birthday Gifts, but Can't Tell Anyone

Happy Birthday to you, lazy girl! It's another special day and another occasion for your family and friends to celebrate who you are and what you mean to them. Unfortunately, as you're discovering through their year's worth of gifts to you, "who you are" includes the following:

- Pusher of Vacuum Apparatus (bagless vacuum)
- Girlfriend in Need of One-Size–Too-Small Lingerie (which could be a good thing depending on how you spin it . . .)
- Person Who Obviously Needs to Give Just a Little Bit More (donation to charity given in your name)

Wow. Talk about some lame gifts! You've almost started to dread the holidays that are supposed to be "about you," because usually they're about you pretending to be delighted by gifts that make you want to regift your entire clan.

You're not ungrateful, really! It's just that you give, and give, and give, all year round. It would be nice if just for these few days, you could receive something awesome.

Lazy Girl Hack: Don't Turn Gifts Into a Test

We all know at least one person who treats gift giving as an unofficial test of love, devotion, respect, or any of those other emotions Hallmark clearly invented. Maybe you are that person. The reality is, gifts aren't a test—they're just gifts. Ideally, we give gifts freely out of love, and accept them gratefully out of love. Sitting around wondering if your boyfriend is going to "get it right" this time is a quick way to end up being very disappointed. So, maybe he gives you a washing machine for Christmas. It's not the most romantic gift, but maybe he was trying to make life easier for you. Or maybe he commits the common male crime of giving you lingerie. Just think—there are women who don't have a guy who *wants* to see them in lingerie. The point here is that you love your family and significant other, and they love you. They've already passed the test. Everything beyond that is a bonus.

You Know You're a Lazy Girl When . . .

You give all your gifts in gift bags because wrapping them is way too much work.

Lazy Girl Hack: Be Nicer to Yourself

It has been my observation that women who place the most emphasis on gifts are those who don't treat themselves right. They are almost martyr-like in their unselfishness all year round, and then when a birthday or holiday rolls around, they think "Finally, a day for me." They inevitably fall into the trap of trying to make up for a year's worth of self-denial in a single day. You can see how that math wouldn't work, right? Naturally, it's not going to be enough, even if your family throws you a parade down Main Street and gets the two not-dead Beatles back together to serenade you.

So you need to treat yourself to the things you want throughout the year. It's almost like what they say about sex: If you know how to please yourself, your partner will know how to please you (actually, they say *pleasure* yourself, but that is the grossest verb ever). Likewise, if you treat yourself to a massage or a nice bottle of perfume once in a while, you'll be less likely to make everything hinge on gifts. Plus, your family will actually start to get an idea of what you like. Your next lingerie gift will be a dominatrix suit and whip!

PROBLEM

You're Having People Over, but Your Apartment Is So Small

Oh, your boyfriend and his big mouth—he went and told all of his friends that the two of you would be hosting the Big Game in your small, small apartment. Your living room, in particular, is tiny and cramped enough to seem like a shoebox diorama, or a Barbie Dreamhouse overrun by beer-swilling, jersey-wearing Ken dolls. The point is that they're going to be so closely packed into your Dreamhouse that they'll be practically falling into the Barbie fireplace. They'll be knocking over the teensy miniature Barbie books on the bookshelf. And as for Barbie—um, I mean you—you'll be squeezed into the corner of the room with your tray of teeny tiny snack foods while your poorly supported doll head partly tips over into the Barbie ironing board.

Okay, so maybe that's an exaggeration, but your living room is small. It's so small that there's only room for a very little bit of living. Time for some quick and easy hacks so you can live large, lazy girl!

Lazy Girl Hack: Clear the Floor

One of the first things you should do to make your living room seem bigger is to get as much stuff off your floor as possible. Take any clutter that might be eating up space and stow it away in boxes. The more your guests can see of the floor, the more "open" the room will look. An open-looking room is going to seem larger. Even statues or plants that might be on the floor should be moved up onto shelves to create more floor space. You can even remove large rugs to make the floor look more spacious, but if that seems like too much work (and it probably does) just vacuum the rug so everything looks clean.

You Know You're a Lazy Girl When . . .
You bought a Roomba, but you only use it for your cat to ride around on in a little shark costume.

Lazy Girl Hack: Keep It Light and Small

Writers at www.trustedpros.com say your décor also plays a role in making your living room look bigger (or smaller). Light, neutral, or bright paint colors tend to make a room look larger—be sure to go with solid colors. Dark colors are not a good idea, since they tend to create that overly cozy, borderline "claustrophobically trapped" look. Patterned wallpaper is also considered a no-no for small rooms.

You should also use furniture that is made to scale for small rooms. Just like the Barbie Dreamhouse utilizes teensy furniture, you should choose small furniture for your small living room. Not quite Barbie small, but as small as can comfortably fit an average human. It's also useful to find any kind of furniture that serves a dual function, such as a cabinet that doubles as a coffee table, or a sofa bed that also has storage compartments.

Lazy Girl Hack: Smoke and Mirrors

Who has the best fake-spacious living room of them all? Quite possibly you, if you put a big, Wicked Queen–style mirror on your wall. A large wall mirror can go a long way toward artificially expanding a small room. Such a mirror is even more effective if you hang it across from something really open and infinite looking, like a fireplace or a window. This will add a sort of endless beauty to the room. Note: Do *not* put the mirror across from your plasma TV with those silly men running around in their tight pants and helmets. That will just create the illusion of endless stupidity. Which is the stupidest sport of them all? We already have the answer.

PROBLEM

Your Friend Is Coming Over for Coffee and Your Kitchen Is in Bad Shape

If your house or apartment were a person, it would be a person with a severe stomach virus, because it's throwing up all over itself. (Or are you purging, little house? Don't you know you're far too small already?) Your kitchen table is spewing old electric bills and coupon circulars so outdated they've practically recycled themselves out of embarrassment. Not to mention those mysterious refrigerator items so furry that you suspect they now have central nervous systems.

Absolutely no one *wants* to clean their kitchen. It's gross. It's labor intensive. And it's smelly—especially if you've been letting it fend for itself for a while. But your friend has been after you for a while to meet up and you can either pull yourself together enough to meet her at the way-too-expensive espresso bar up near her house (at least a half an hour away) or you can suck it up and half-ass a kitchen clean. People like to know that their food and beverages are being prepared in an *E. coli*–free environment, so if you choose the latter, here's how to get through it without putting in too much effort.

Lazy Girl Hack: Clear Your Counters

Space gives the illusion of cleanliness, so even if you don't have the time, energy, or desire to do a total clean (which we all know you don't), you should clean the crap off your counters.

Believe it or not, your kitchen is not actually the best place for your laptop, last week's newspaper, the unfolded laundry, or that birthday gift for your niece that you haven't gotten a chance to mail yet. Assess the items on your counters. Do all of them belong there? If not, gather these items into a box, and stuff them into a cabinet or closet for the day. (No, unfortunately, you cannot "box and banish" your guests.)

Lazy Girl Hack: Ditch the Dirty Dishes

There's no way to hide a sink full of dirty dishes, but you don't really have time to clean them. And honestly, how much does your back hurt when you stand at the sink for that long anyway? Fortunately, if you have a dishwasher, you should be in good shape. Take all those dirty dishes and hide the crap out of them in the dishwasher. Even if some items aren't dishwasher-safe, hide them in there anyway. At least they're out of the way and you can put them right back in the sink (to "soak," right?) once your company's gone. Just don't forget to go back and either run a cycle or get the dishes out of there. The last thing you need is to go through this a month or two from now and find a festering load of dirty dishes.

You Know You're a Lazy Girl When . . .

You consider it an injustice that you need to prerinse the dishes before putting them into the dishwasher. (Sounds like dishwashers are lazy girls too!)

If your dishwasher is already full of dirty dishes just run it already. At least your friend will know that you're trying. And if you don't have a dishwasher, throw some dish soap in there and run the water until the soap bubbles cover up all the dishes. If you do this right before your company arrives, no one will be the wiser!

Lazy Girl Hack: Face the Fridge

Finally, it's time to face the fridge monsters. Begin by burning some potpourri or cinnamon sticks on the stove, and get ready to get rid of anything that festers (other than your boyfriend).

The best thing to do is take everything out of your fridge and clean it before putting anything back in. But that seems like it's going to take way too long. So just do a shelf at a time. Remove all the items from one shelf and wipe it down. Once that's done, start sorting. Throw away anything that's expired or questionable and let go of items that you know you'll never eat. Next, take inventory of the items that remain and decide how you'll organize them. Keep similar items together. Take full advantage of the drawers, shelves, and refrigerator door.

If your fridge smells, don't feel too bad. Think of everything you keep in your fridge: fish, yesterday's takeout, burritos, cat food, curry, cheese, and plenty of items that are just waiting for next week's trash day, like just-past-its-expiration-date milk, fruit, and so on. You name it . . . it's stored in your fridge. An easy way to solve this problem is to stick an open container or box of baking soda in the back of your fridge. The baking soda will suck up the majority of smells and keep your fridge smelling like a dream—or at least not something you're afraid to face.

PROBLEM

Your Friend Wants You to Volunteer at Her Charity, but You're Not Feeling It

Remember that friend who forced you to pretend to make homemade baked goods for her fundraiser? Apparently she really doesn't get that all you want to do in your free time is hang out on your couch because now she's harassing you about volunteering at her charity. She hosts events all. the. time. And she always wants you to come and help out. Unfortunately, at some point you're going to have to suck it up and go volunteer, but with these hacks, you can absolutely make sure your friend isn't asking you all the time.

Lazy Girl Hack: Do Something Occasionally

Although you definitely don't want to go to your friend's events, you're going to have to occasionally put in an appearance for friendship's sake. When this happens, be sure to choose an event that you might possibly find tolerable, and show up with a smile on your face.

You might think this erratic participation will hurt you, but I beg to differ. Think about the guys you dated when you were younger. Who was the guy that you were most hung up on? Was it the guy who never ever called you after the first date? Or was it the guy who called you occasionally, then ignored you, then reappeared and called you out of the blue? I'm betting it was that second guy. This is called "intermittent reinforcement," and it's an actual thing. It's used in dog training and slot machines. People keep feeding money into a slot machine based on very occasional, random payouts. That's like what you'll be—an occasional, random payout. Jackpot!

Lazy Girl Hack: Use Your Phone

This may not be the best idea if you want to maintain a close friendship with your do-gooder, but it's a great way to get out of something that you were forced into. Take "important business calls" at the bake sale, argue with your colleagues about the upcoming merger at the PTA meeting, or book a flight to Kuala Lumpur for an upcoming convention at the Sunday school fundraiser. It doesn't necessarily matter if these calls are real; they can be from a friend posing as a work call. But just take them, take a lot of them, and give them priority over the activity at hand. I know, this type of person with the "important cell phone call" is annoying, but that's the whole idea. If you present yourself as that creepy career mom at the bake sale with more of a Bluetooth than a sweet tooth, they most likely won't have you back.

PROBLEM

Your Bathroom Is Disgusting and Your Parents Are on Their Way Over

The bathroom: everyone's least favorite room to clean. Honestly, they're not that bad. Bathrooms are among the smaller rooms in the house, and they generally don't attract much clutter that doesn't belong there. But with all the toiletries, linens, and cleaning products that can accumulate, it's a space that can easily get out of control—and fast! And now your parents are on their way over and you just know your mom is going to judge you for your grimy shower and your dad is going to comment on the toothpaste splatter on the mirror. However, with these hacks, you can stop panicking and make your bathroom presentable, if not exactly "clean."

Lazy Girl Hack: Clean Yourself and Your Tub at the Same Time

About to hop in the shower and give yourself a scrub? Why not do the same for your tub? Cleaning the tub while you're in it anyway is a great way to lessen the pain of bathroom maintenance. Just be sure you're using an all-natural, odorless cleaner; you don't want to pass out from toxic fumes and hit your head on the faucet.

Then someone else will have a mess to clean up! Or, if you're taking a bath instead of a shower, just dump about a quarter of a box of baking soda into your bathwater; this will soothe your sore muscles and clean the tub at the same time.

In the future, consider keeping a squeegee in the shower. It's a great way to prevent bathroom moisture from turning into hard-to-remove mold and mildew. Just keep one in a cabinet or drawer near the tub, and squeegee the tile walls and/or glass doors after every shower. The squeegee will wipe the water off the walls and send it down to the drain where it belongs.

Lazy Girl Hack: Swap Out the Shower Curtain

Take a look at your shower curtain. Does anything strike you? If you have a nasty mold situation, torn shower curtain ring holes, or a shower curtain you just dislike, now's the time to start fresh. It's a fact that nothing makes a bathroom seem cleaner than it is than the chemical smell of a new shower curtain . . . especially if yours is way late for the trash can. So tear your gross one out of the shower and get that new one up quick. Mom and Dad will be so impressed that this is taken care of that they might not notice the toothpaste smeared in the sink.

Going forward, replace your regular curtain with a sturdy, mildew-resistant shower curtain liner, pick up a bottle of shower cleaner—or just use watered-down bleach—and spray on the inside of the curtain after each use to keep mold at bay.

Lazy Girl Hack: Use Your Dirty Clothes to Clean Up

Let's be honest, if you're like most lazy girls, your bathroom floor is probably covered in dirty clothes. And your sink and vanity are probably covered in a thin layer of dust. If you're half-assing a bathroom cleanup, use those dirty clothes to your advantage and wipe down whatever you can with them before throwing them into your washing machine or hamper, or just shoving them into an already full closet that you know no one will dare to open. Sure, wiping down your bathroom with your clothes is kind of gross, but so is having a dirty bathroom in the first place. At least you up the chances of actually doing a load of laundry if you really can't wear your clothes again.

Lazy Girl Hack: Light a Candle Already

As you know, bathrooms can get a little dank and smelly from time to time—which is why you're scrambling to make yours presentable now. Luckily, you can pretend that this room is nice and fresh by turning off the lights and firing up a candle instead. The low light will hide any dirt or grime you haven't been able to wipe down and the smell will both mask any gross smell that you haven't been able to eliminate and make your guests think that you're keeping up on your housework. If you don't have scented candles, try incense, a plug-in air freshener, or even some really fragrant fresh-cut flowers if you're in a pinch.

PROBLEM

You've Been Living It Up in Your Living Room—and It Shows

Ah, the living room. Your home inside your home. The place you spend so much time in that your butt has imprinted itself perfectly in your couch and Netflix is always spot-on with its viewing recommendations. Unfortunately, you spend so much time in your living room that it really looks like you only live in that room. Maybe your roommates are starting to complain about the way your nail polish, magazines, and dirty laundry have taken over the common space. Or maybe you have guests coming over who don't want to feel like they're invading your personal space just by sitting on the couch. Either way, you need to find a way to appease those who just aren't as comfortable with the time you spend in the living room as you are.

Lazy Girl Hack: Just Say Spray

The number one lazy girl solution to any cleaning problem? Air freshener. If a place *smells* clean, it must *be* clean, right? Even if that's not necessarily true, you can still make your roommates and your guests feel more at home by making sure your home doesn't just smell like you.

The trick is to do more than just spray the air. That smell will go away way too quickly! Instead, spray your furniture. Spray your rugs. Spray your pillows and throw blankets and everything else you can to ensure the smell will stick around. An even better way to make this work? Go to your local home goods store and find the beach/summer aisle. Don't get distracted by beach balls and Slip 'N Slides. Instead, pick up a spray bottle with a fan attachment on the end. These are usually battery powered and are meant for spritzing yourself with water to cool down at the beach. When you get home, unscrew the fan attachment and screw it onto your bottle or air freshener, or simply pour some air freshener into the bottle you just purchased. Then walk around your living room dispensing bursts of freshness!

Lazy Girl Hack: Dust Just Enough

Dusting is a key part of making sure your living room is clean, but it really takes way too much work. You have to lift everything up, dust underneath it, put everything back. If you can't find that kind of motivation—and who the hell can?—don't worry. All you really have to do is dust the tops of things (with a feather duster, microfiber cloths, etc.) and no one will be the wiser. As a bonus, you'll not only get rid of dust, you'll make the room smell clean to boot. Feel free to dust baseboards and corners with a duster that has a pole. You'll save time—and your back.

Also, you may have noticed that lampshades get dustier more quickly than almost any other surface in the house. They're like dust magnets, and traditional dusting tools don't seem to do a thing. Don't even bother with dusters. If you find yourself overly concerned about dust on your lampshades, go find your lint roller or lint brush. If you don't have one, go to any home goods store and pick one up. There are two common styles: one with disposable adhesive sheets and another that you clean by hand and use over and over. Either is fine. Once you've got it, roll your lampshade the way you would a garment to remove dust, lint, and pet hair. It works like a charm!

Lazy Girl Hack: Suck It Up

Vacuuming isn't the most thrilling chore in the world, but every once in a while you just have to do it. This is certainly the case when company is coming over; your guests don't need to tread on crumbs from movie popcorn, scraps from your last craft project, and dirt tracked in on the soles of shoes. And nothing, absolutely nothing, makes a room look cleaner than a freshly vacuumed floor. So if you really want to shoot for the stars, pull out that pain-in-the-ass Hoover and get to work. But don't go overboard.

If you have a rug on the floor, start there. Move the coffee table but not the couch, and pay special attention to the areas where people walk and where crumbs might fall to the floor. As for the rest of the room, stick to the traffic areas; don't even think about moving the TV cabinet! If there are dust bunnies back there, they're small and no one else is going to see them.

PROBLEM

Your Bedroom's a Disaster and You're Hoping to Have Company

Your bedroom is your sanctuary. The place where you rest your head and, unfortunately, keep all the crap that you can't keep in the other rooms of your house or apartment. Well, you have a date tonight that you hope will end with breakfast tomorrow morning, but it's not a sure thing so you don't want to put too much effort into cleaning up. Fortunately, you can fake a clean bedroom without a ton of effort. Save that energy for tonight, lazy girl!

Lazy Girl Hack: Make Your Bed

Remember when Mom used to force you to make your bed each morning? She wasn't trying to torture you; she was onto something. Your bed is the central object in this room, so its condition will automatically rub off on everything around it. A nicely made bed promotes a feeling of calm in your bedroom, which will in turn rub off on you! Of course, some days are busier than others, and you won't always have time to do a perfect job of it. On those occasions, just pull up the covers and straighten the pillows.

And, don't think that a nicely made bed will make up for sheets that haven't been changed in months. So if you're having company over, please—we beg you—change your sheets!

Lazy Girl Hack: Rise above It

If you've already done some purging in your bedroom but you find you still don't have enough space for your belongings, it's time to take your storage strategy to the next level, literally. Go to your local home goods store and pick up a set of bed risers. These are wooden or plastic blocks that go beneath the four legs of your bed, raising it higher and creating more space underneath it. These extra inches allow you to store (and hide) plastic storage containers, shoeboxes, suitcases—items that you don't need at the ready at all times but that you want to hide when you're letting someone in your bedroom for the first time.

You Know You're a Lazy Girl When . . .

You have company coming over and you only clean the rooms you know people will go into.

If you do decide to go with bed risers, you may also want to invest in a bed ruffle (also called a bed skirt). It's essentially a little curtain that keeps the space under your bed hidden from view, allowing you to fully utilize your newfound storage space. If you get one that matches your bedding, it will add an extra aesthetic touch without much extra effort. All you do is spread out the dust ruffle between your mattress and box spring. Just make sure you get one long enough to hide your under-the-bed storage.

Lazy Girl Hack: Get a Room Divider

If you've hidden stuff under your bed and your bedroom is still overrun with clutter, it's time to take things to the next level. Get all of your stuff out of sight and out of mind by using a screen or room divider, or by hanging a curtain around your bed. That way, when you enter the sleeping area, you can put all other thoughts behind you—literally.

Lazy Girl Hack: Use a Secret Sachet

We've talked a lot about how smell can make anything seem inviting and it works in your bedroom too. If you don't have time or a desire to do a deep clean on your bedroom, just slip a sachet inside each of your pillowcases. You can buy premade sachets at most home goods and department stores, or if you feel especially motivated you can make your own. To do this, first go to a crafts store and buy some potpourri. Choose a scent that you find comforting, such as apple cinnamon or honey vanilla. Then take a pair of old nylons and cut them at the ankle. Fill the nylons three-quarters of the way with potpourri and then tie them off. Once they're in the pillowcases you won't be able to see them, but you will smell the difference!

If you really don't feel like putting any effort in, just use air freshener. Linen and upholstery fresheners, such as Febreze, offer an easy way to give your bedroom a clean feel without lifting a finger. Simply spray your comforter and pillows and any upholstered furniture in the room, and take a whiff. Smells like you just did laundry, right? There are also special closet sprays that keep hanging clothes fresh and aromatherapy linen sprays for use on your pillows before you get into bed at night. Lavender is a calming scent that is commonly used to promote deep, restful sleep. Just spray your pillow, give it a few moments to work its way into the fibers of the fabric, and then lay down your weary head. By morning you'll feel completely refreshed—and so will your bedroom!

PROBLEM

Your Home Office Is a Mess, but You're Meeting a New Client

You're one of the lucky ones—either you're able to work from home or you run your own business out of your home office. Either way, if you're a lazy girl working from home, chances are good that your home office suffers from at least a little bit of neglect. Normally, this is totally fine. You work by yourself. No one sees your yoga pants or the shape of your office. But every so often, you have a client who wants to meet on your home turf and panic ensues. It's not an issue if you follow these hacks . . .

Lazy Girl Hack: Let the Sunshine In!

If you have windows in your office, pull up the blinds! You may think that adding more light will just show all the flaws, but it will actually make the client feel relaxed and at home.

If the raw sunlight is too bright, pick up some sheer curtains, which will soften the light without blocking it out completely. Consider various options when choosing lamps, lighting fixtures, and light bulbs for your office. For example, fluorescent light bulbs may be cheaper and last longer, but they're much tougher on your eyes (and your mood) than traditional light bulbs. Plus, part of the luxury of working from home is that you can be productive without being forced to function in an industrial environment.

Seize the freedom you have and make your office ideally suited to your own needs—and make cleaning up for your clients easy on everyone.

You Know You're a Lazy Girl When . . .
You run a business and you are your own laziest employee.

Lazy Girl Hack: Clean Off Your Desk

It doesn't matter if you have (neatly stacked) piles of paperwork on the floor or a plant that's in need of a little water on your file cabinet. As long as your desk is clean, you're really in good shape and the rest can be seen as a sign of how busy you are. But, honestly, cleaning off your desk takes time and you don't have much to spare. So if you have an unexpected client coming in, just grab some boxes or bins or baskets and go to town. Then wipe down your desk and you're good to go!

PART 5

Dragging Yourself Through the Workday

Ugh, work! It's a perfect encapsulation of all the things that lazy girls hate the most. You have to set an alarm, abandon your amazingly comfortable bed, and look like you've showered and are wearing clean clothes. Then you have to rush to make it to work on time, just to spend the whole day . . . working. *It's. the. worst.* The worst! Fortunately, that same bed awaits you at the end of a long day and the hacks in this part will help you do everything from staying awake during that late-afternoon meeting to pretending you know what you're doing when you absolutely don't to interacting with your obnoxious coworkers. So read on . . . and get to work, lazy girl!

PROBLEM

It's a Perfect Beach Day, but You're Supposed to Work

Remember when you were a kid and you used to hold that old-school thermometer up to a scorching hot light bulb in order to get a day off from school? Sure, the thermometer melted and exploded into a zillion liquid metallic pieces in your hand, but that exposure to poisonous mercury was still enough to worry your mom. Mission accomplished!

Ah, how you long for those simple days of sick trickery. Now that you're a grownup, you have responsibilities, and your boss expects you to handle them in a mature and professional way. Plus, melting a digital thermometer just leaves you with a bunch of cheap, gooey plastic.

The truth is, there is not a single person in the universe who hasn't faked being sick, or at least wanted to. Faux sickness is an accepted reality and not a huge deal, but you need to handle it right. No one wants to be able to see right through a lame facade, so meet your boss halfway and try to be convincing.

Lazy Girl Hack: Lie, but Remember That Less Is More

When calling in sick, your first instinct might be to go into grotesque detail about your faux illness. While I'm sure your boss would love to hear your colorful description of how squid ink pasta looks after digestion, resist the urge. Overexplanation reeks of lying. Besides, the more details you give, the more details you'll have to remember. Keep it as general and simple as possible. If you absolutely can't bear the idea of just saying, "I'm sick today," use general categories such as "sore throat," "stomach flu," or "fever." If you can avoid it, though, don't say "cold." Why? Well . . .

Lazy Girl Hack: Don't Say "Cold"

Sure, you know that having a bad head cold makes you a wretched, socially unacceptable creature, with a runny, hideously inflamed nose so red it could put old Rudolph out of work. Actually, you might want to inquire into that position because if you call in at work too often for colds, you're going to be jobless. It's one of those weird things in life: Everyone knows colds suck huge, but we all pretend they're no big deal. They just don't count as a "real" sickness. Never mind the fact that a recent study found that driving with a cold is comparable to driving drunk (even without the heavily spiked cold meds). If you tell your boss that you have a horrible case of the sniffles, you are going to sound wussier than the lead singer of an emo band.

Lazy Girl Hack: Use Your Feminine Wiles

Okay, now I'm going to let you in on a little bit of an unfair double standard—and this one actually works in our favor! If you have a male boss, the all-powerful "female problems" explanation continues to be a timeless get-out-of-jail-free card. Uttering those words to a male boss will make him want to get off the phone with you as quickly as possible, throw up a little in his mouth, and not talk to you again until you stop having female problems. It's a beautiful thing. Imagine a guy calling in with male problems! The very phrase is laughable—and possibly redundant. Men *are* a male problem; the least they can do is come to work.

Lazy Girl Hack: Avoid Being Obvious

There are some days—such as Mondays, Fridays, and the day after the Super Bowl—when a sick excuse will never be believed. I repeat: Will. Not. Be. Believed. Even if it's the truth, the whole truth, and nothing but. On days like this, you can bet yours won't be the only message on Bossy McBosserson's voice mail. People are predictable that way, and you don't want to be predictable. So unless you are truly feeling awful, try to avoid taking sick days that scream "early weekend" (Friday), "epic hangover" (Monday), or "suspiciously tan" (obscenely gorgeous day). Although if you happen to be the type who burns instead of tans, a day spent in the sun can double nicely as a fever flush. Good for you, Lobster Girl!

You Know You're a Lazy Girl When . . .
You're annoyed by how far into the ocean you have to wade in order to hide the fact that you're peeing in it.

PROBLEM

You're Supposed to Be Working from Home, but What You Really Want to Do Is Relax

The truth is, your company is the kind of place where you're actually glad to show up every day—or not show up. Because you have a long, painful commute, your boss actually lets you have a couple of days a week to "work from home." It's this kind of flexibility and trust in your work ethic that makes you a happy and dedicated member of the team. If only more employers would stop hovering and entrust employees with the freedom to make their own schedules, there would be a much happier workforce overall.

Of course, "work from home" for you really means "eat Chocolate Cheerios in your pajamas while watching TV and playing online all day." Wait—that's not really fair. It doesn't always mean that. Sometimes, it means "go to the beach, lie around, and get fried by the sun while eating curly cheese fries until 5:00 p.m."

But you don't want your *boss* to know that, especially since your company is so cool and flexible about that stuff. You need to present the illusion that you are actually having something resembling a normal workday from your home. This work-from-home thing is just too awesome to screw up!

Lazy Girl Hack: Send Scheduled Emails

Did you know that you don't have to be at your desk—or even on your smartphone—to send emails during the slavish hours of nine to five? There are apps, such as Boomerang for Gmail, that allow you to schedule messages for hours, days, even up to a month in advance. So if you need to turn in an assignment or update your boss on a certain project, but would really rather take a nice long nap in front of the TV at that time, just schedule your email to be sent at the designated time and nap away.

Did I say nine to five? Why restrict yourself to normal working hours? We all know you can be *so* much more productive if you start working at 6:00 a.m.! Schedule a whole slew of emails to be sent at 6:00 a.m, and you will look like the most ambitious early-bird freak on the planet. People will get to their desks at 8:00 a.m. and feel sheepish because of you. Way to go!

Of course, in order to keep up with the responses to these messages, you will need to check your email at some point in the day. But checking email a few times a day is a lot better than actually monitoring your incoming messages all day long like you're at work.

You Know You're a Lazy Girl When . . .
You work from home and clean pajamas make up your entire work wardrobe.

Lazy Girl Hack: Save Up Work from Previous Days

When you're actually at the office, you don't *always* have to produce a final product to convince your boss you are working—just shuffling papers and typing a lot can do that job pretty well. However, when you're working from home, you can shuffle all the papers you want and type until your fingers are numb, but if your boss can't see it, it doesn't count.

Nope, you should save the shuffling and typing for when it can be seen, and stockpile your actual output for work-from-home days. That way, you can turn in a bunch of stuff on those days even while you're watching old *Full House* reruns. It will look like you're even *more* productive on work-from-home days than on shuffle-and-type days!

Okay, the truth is, you're going to have to break down and work at some point during the week, otherwise, the stuff is never going to get done. But if you work smart, not hard, you can still have plenty of time left over to do nothing at all.

PROBLEM

You're Totally Unqualified for a Job, but Apply Anyway

So, you saw a listing for your dream job and you can't wait to apply. You've envisioned your new life with this amazing job—your days would be a delirious haze of nonstop excitement, achievement, and paycheck spending. There's just one teensy problem—you're not exactly qualified for this job. At all.

Believe it or not, you can present yourself well even if you aren't a perfect match for the job. It's just a matter of looking good on paper! Check out these hacks to learn how to put the least amount of energy into your resume and still get job interviews like a rockstar.

Lazy Girl Hack: Don't Overcompensate!

At some point in this process, you might have thought to yourself, "Okay, so I'm not qualified—I'll just make up for that with lots of fancy fonts and a super cool layout. That'll do it."

As great as that sounds, I'm here to tell you that business professionals tend not to like "fun" fonts, emoticons, or crazy layouts—at least not in a resume. You can't just make them forget that you have no experience by distracting them with pretty, shiny things, okay? That's what the *interview* is for. For the resume, simply show your seriousness and professionalism with a simple black-and-white document, no cutesy stuff.

Lazy Girl Hack: Don't Pad—Lift!

There's a difference between a padded bra and a pushup bra: A padded bra adds synthetic stuffing to your natural endowments, while a pushup bra gently lifts and accentuates what you already have. So it should be with your resume: You want a "pushup" resume.

If you don't have relevant work experience, you should list any extracurricular activities or volunteer work you have done in that area. Otherwise, list all jobs and extracurricular activities where you've used the Universal Skills: dealing with humans, writing, speaking, and reading. These are skills we all use daily, and they can be applied to most any job. You might want to present your experience through a "functional resume" rather than a "chronological resume." Instead of listing your jobs in chronological order, list your most relevant experience first.

In the meantime, between jobs, it's always smart to cultivate other interests or hobbies through organized projects or clubs. You might be able to use the experiences and skills learned from participating in them on a future application.

Lazy Girl Hack: Express Yourself Well

Communication skills are fundamental to almost any job, so it's essential that you use good grammar, punctuation, and spelling on your resume. A killer cover letter is also a great way to catch the interest of a hiring manager. If you present yourself as a dynamic, articulate person who can communicate well, you'll increase your chances of getting any job. Special note: If you are sending out multiple resumes or cover letters, *please* be sure to customize your materials for each specific job. You would be surprised at how many people send out "form resumes" and cover letters without updating them to suit the job in question. It might be easier for *you* to send out a letter telling a grade school that you'd be "great at training their animals," but it might hurt your chances of landing an interview. Oh well, envelopes for dinner again!

PROBLEM

You Have Zero Relevant Job Experience, but Still Scored an Interview

Hooray! You've been called in for an interview for a job you know you would love and that you are pretty sure you'd be great at. The job's meant for you, and you are meant for it—it's true love! Now it's just a matter of convincing this intimidatingly tall, perfectly coiffed hiring manager not to stand between you and your true love.

Why would she do that? Well, if we're being honest here, you don't exactly have the precise work experience that the job calls for. In fact, you have zero relevant job experience and have pretty much only worked a series of proverbial "odd jobs." Some of them have been truly odd too—dressing up as Elsa for kids' parties, being a hair washer at a salon, renting yourself out as a human guinea pig for pharmaceutical drug trials, and, of course, writing fortune cookies.

But don't be discouraged. You might not have experience in the field, but you may very well have the skill set the job requires. For example, you're a self-starter, you're able to work independently, you have excellent people skills, and you're comfortable in a fast-paced environment. So, why should it matter how you acquired these skills? A wise man once said, "There is more than one journey toward any destination." Actually, you wrote that for a fortune cookie once.

Lazy Girl Hack: Market Your "Brand"

The fact that you've been brought in for an interview is a very encouraging sign. Obviously, these people saw something on your resume that prompted them to make time in their schedules to meet you. For this reason, you should focus more on being personable and charming than on whatever's missing from your job history. Remember, they've already seen your resume and they called you anyway. What they haven't seen is *you.* So show them some you! Make sure you look like a million bucks, or at least a hundred thousand. Smile and let your personality show, but keep it professional. It's great to showcase your wit and charm, but don't try to turn this thing into a one-woman monologue. Keep it succinct and let the interviewer control the direction and the pace of the conversation.

Lazy Girl Hack: Don't Overexplain Yourself

You might feel compelled to justify your lack of relevant job experience. All I can say is *don't do it.* You don't need to address this topic unless they bring it up. Do *not* offer lengthy or unrequested explanations for any gaps or oddities in your resume. In fact, I'd say for life in general, *overexplaining yourself is a horrible idea*, no matter how tempting it is. It's like a rabbit hole of insecurity that you'll only fall deeper and deeper into. Next thing you know, you'll want to explain why you're explaining so much, and so on, and so on, until they call those nice men to escort you out.

Lazy Girl Hack: Use What You Have

As I mentioned previously, there's more than one way to skin a cat, although if you ever had a job as a cat skinner, I don't ever want to talk to you again.

The point is, whether you know it or not, you do have a skill set. It doesn't matter if the jobs you've had were weird; they taught you something. Dressing up as Elsa for kids' parties gave you skills in entertainment, party planning, and self-motivation. Plus, there were some communication skills involved, not to mention the fast-paced environment. (Boy, did you have to move fast to avoid those kids trying to smother you to death!) Being a human guinea pig taught you to take risks, and writing fortune cookies taught you innovation and intuition. A job as a janitor teaches organization and attention to detail, and being a pool lifeguard teaches how to look good in sunglasses while pretending to watch kids. Believe me, this is a skill you'll need if you decide to become a parent!

PROBLEM

You Hate Your Job, but Can't Quit

You weren't sure what you were going to do with that English degree when you graduated college, but you sure as hell didn't plan on becoming a "Management Facilitation Implementation Coordinator" for a "Business Matrix Resource Strategic Compliance Corporation." (Note: If reading this job description did not put you to sleep, you might be okay without this advice.) But, hey, you've got to eat—at least that's what they always say. Although after eating lunch in that gray cubicle, you're feeling dangerously close to taking a nap on your spreadsheets.

Let's be honest. You may hate your job, but acting like you hate it isn't going to get you anywhere. And it's much easier to feign enthusiasm than it is to stress out because your boss wants to talk about how unenthused you actually are.

Lazy Girl Hack: Show Up

Here's the thing about faking enthusiasm for a soul-crushing corporate job: you've won half the battle just by showing up. A corporation is kind of like a guy who's clueless in bed—full of itself, fascinated by the sound of its own voice, and utterly selfish (although, hopefully, your workplace will last longer than thirty seconds). Just think about how easy it is to fake it with that kind of guy. That's because with his inflated sense of self-worth, he naturally *assumes* you are having the time of your life. And if you're actually not? *He doesn't really care* because you're there anyway. As long as he has his fun and you make the right noises, all is right in his world.

That's kind of how it is with a boring corporate job. They've got you, they know it, and it doesn't make much difference to them if you're living your lifelong dream or if you die a little inside each time you swipe your ID badge. But they *do* expect you to make a convincing show of *pretending*. Beyond doing the actual job efficiently, this entails projecting a certain level of faux enthusiasm.

Lazy Girl Hack: Communicate via Email

To make it easier on yourself, you should do as much faking as you can over email. In the world of email, emotions can be hidden behind emoticons. (I hate you with a seething passion, becomes a smiley face. You're completely inept, becomes a wink.) Likewise, boredom can be masked with jargon. (Zzzzz becomes: With respect to key performance indicators, our team promises a fast turnaround on all deliverables.) Take full advantage of all email opportunities—you're very lucky to be living in an era tailor-made for lazy girls. Just think of the pre-email working stiffs of the past—like the employees on *Mad Men*, for example. If they needed to fake enthusiasm, they had to drink a Scotch on the rocks.

You Know You're a Lazy Girl When . . .
Your password to log in to all of your accounts is the same.

Lazy Girl Hack: Face It—and Fake It

Sometimes, despite your truly brilliant email dispatches, you will be called upon to convey enthusiasm using your actual voice and face. In such situations, you'll need to step up your game a bit. Rule number one is—smile! Don't even worry about whether your smile looks false. There are a lot of fake smiles in the world, and worrying about it will only make it more strained. As long as it involves the corners of your mouth being pulled upward in an arc formation, you're a success.

Same with your voice—don't sweat whether you sound 100 percent genuine. If when you say, "That win-win is outside the box!" you aim for "psychotically excited," your natural apathy will probably bring you down to "reasonably and nonfreakishly interested." Perfect!

These tips come with one important caveat: Don't get *too* good at faking, especially when it comes to a job you can't stand. When working your faux mojo at a soul-crushing job, these hacks should be a quick fix, not a long-term solution. Life is short. If you are bored senseless by this job, you should start plotting an escape route. Answer some ads, network online, and go to job fairs. Even if it means going back to school and giving up some fun and some sleep, isn't that better than falling asleep at your desk every day? Think of these lazy hacks as being like a prescription painkiller—you can use it for a while, but don't become a junkie. Deal?

PROBLEM

Your Coworkers Are So Boring, but You Have to Pretend to Be Interested

First there was your office's resident Bridezilla, who happens to work two cubicles away from you, and whose voice can be heard shrilly arguing with wedding planners about origami swans vs. live butterflies, chicken satay vs. crab cakes, and which creepily oedipal song she should dance to with her father. You thought that was bad enough.

Then the woman who sits next to you got engaged. Now everywhere she goes, female shrieks can be heard in reaction to the gigantic, twenty-four-karat monstrosity she's lugging around on her finger. Her new job title seems to be "Interoffice Diamond-Showing Liaison," and she's good at it. She won't rest until every single person in the building has beheld the emerald-cut hunk of radiance that symbolizes her love. You've nicknamed her Ring Kong, and you fantasize about "Ring Kong vs. Bridezilla," an epic showdown to the death fueled only by uncooked rice and Save the Date cards. Awesome.

Then, of course, there's Preggy Peggy, who can't stop showing everyone her ultrasound pics and who details her desire for an unmedicated water birth to whoever will listen.

Really, you wish these ladies well—honest! You just wish you didn't have to hear every detail of their marital and reproductive futures. Sorry, but you do. You totally do. You don't want to be the girl in the office who doesn't care about anyone, so you need to use these hacks to help you out.

Lazy Girl Hack: Pretend She's a Reality Show

You've watched reality shows about crazy wedding dramas, conflicts, and pettiness, right? Well, you have one right in your office now. Sure, everything's all shiny and new at the start, but by the time these girls get to the altar, they will have been dragged through a self-imposed hell that is truly like no other. You'll get to overhear Bridezilla crying into the phone about how she "failed" her latest dress fitting, or interrogating her fiancé about his strange new attachment to the gag blowup doll he got at his bachelor party. (*She* would have no trouble with the dress fitting! She can just deflate!) You can listen to Ring Kong despairing about finding a wedding ring worthy of her beautiful engagement ring, or lamenting the carpal tunnel syndrome she's acquired from its bone-crushing weight. You can sympathize with Preggy Peggy over her worries that her baby will suffer from "nipple confusion." You can't make stuff like this up, and really, it is priceless. You have a three-ring circus going on in your office! How could you *not* be interested? Sit back and enjoy the show!

Lazy Girl Hack: Discuss Current Events

If reality TV isn't your thing, you can always meet halfway and bring the conversation around to something that does interest you, like current events. For example, you can talk to Ring Kong about her fancy ring and how Liberian warlords probably used it to wage civil unrest and commit atrocious crimes against humanity. It'll be so educational! You all can sit around and discuss how pretty diamonds like hers enabled the Revolutionary United Front to force children into becoming soldiers before they even lost all their baby teeth. But it's so sparkly!

Okay, maybe don't go that far, but asking some timely questions about weddings will help you out.

Lazy Girl Hack: Walk in Her Shoes

Okay, if you're not into reality TV *or* current events, I'm not sure what's left. I mean, I think I've covered most network and cable TV programming.

You might just have to fall back on the golden rule: "Do unto others as you would have them do unto you." Remember, at some point, it might be you making the Big Plans. And although you are absolutely certain you would never do unto others any of the wacko nonsense these women have done unto you, try to empathize. You would want people to at least seem interested, right? It's nice to know your coworkers care about an important milestone in your life. Especially if that milestone happens to be a princess cut with fifty-eight facets that may have financed an entire insurgency in Zimbabwe.

PROBLEM

You Don't Feel Like Working, but Have to Seem Busy

Maybe it's a really gorgeous day outside, or maybe you're in a huge fight with your significant other, or maybe you are incredibly tired, sick, hungover, or distracted. Or perhaps it's the simple fact that the garish wattage of the fluorescent lights, the gray, institutional carpeting, and the sickly glow of your computer screen are just not igniting your motivation like they usually do. The writing is on the wall: You're going to be useless today. You could try to fight it, but frankly, you don't want to. The best you can do is to be a warm body in a chair.

Here's the good news—if you're a warm body in a chair, you've won half the battle. Few things bring supervisors more delight than glancing around a room and seeing warm bodies installed in every chair, feverishly faux-working. It doesn't matter if your brain is about as sharp as strained baby food. If you're shuffling papers around in an important-looking way, you're playing a valuable part in maintaining the company image.

I should qualify this by saying that if you have an actual deadline to produce something today, you'll need to suck it up and do it. As far as I know, there's no way to fake actual output, unless you get someone else to do your work for you. And if you're the kind of genius who can get someone else to do your job, you don't need me!

Lazy Girl Hack: Write a Lot of Notes

One great way to seem like you're incredibly busy at work is to plaster your computer monitor/work area with notes. This makes it seem as though you have a great deal of important things going on and that you are very industrious about keeping track of them. Although the notes don't necessarily have to pertain to a real project, they should at least be relevant enough so that if your boss zooms in for a closer look, they make sense. Every once in a while, pull one of them off, study it for a long time, and then start typing for a while (no one will know that you're actually just entering your vacation research into your travel spreadsheet). Eventually, you can discard the note, which suggests you've finished the task described on it.

Lazy Girl Hack: Type, Type, Type

A very tried-and-true method of seeming productive is to type. A lot. Typing, especially if it is done in a brisk and secretarial manner, trumps paper shuffling in these increasingly paperless times. The sound of typing is like the pleasant white noise of an office environment, and it makes bosses happy to hear it . . . even if you are typing an email to your best friend about how much you hate seeing all your favorite movies turned into remakes.

Word of caution: Some bosses, occasionally, actually want to know what you're typing. They'll walk by to just casually see if they can bust you typing a Facebook status, an email, or an eBay bid. For this reason, I suggest typing emails in a Microsoft Word document first, then stealthily pasting them into your email when they're done. If your boss walks by and you're typing away in a Word document, it's doubtful he or she will look closer.

Lazy Girl Hack: Use Camouflage

It used to be that we developed new technologies to make life more efficient. Now, we've reached a point where we're so efficient, we need technologies just to slow stuff down. Enter the Internet—the most wonderful time-suck since the invention of sleeping.

In fact, there are several websites designed to "camouflage" time-wasting computer games in a "professional"-looking screen. One of the more brilliant of these, www.cantyouseeimbusy.com, encrypts various video games in spreadsheet or day planner formats. The games have titles like "Leadership," "Cost Cutter," and "Crash Planning" and can even be customized with your company's name. All of this looks about as interesting as an accountant's dreams and is unlikely to raise even the slightest suspicion in a boss who happens to stop by. In fact, all the migraine-y "charts" and "graphs" will likely drive your boss away, both out of trust in your work ethic and because of his sudden need for a nap. Okay, back to Spreadsheet Space Invaders!

PROBLEM

You're So Tired, but Have to Make It Through One More Boring Meeting

It's 2:00 p.m., and if you were living in a much more awesome country with a more laid-back culture, you'd be taking a siesta. After a heavy midday meal, full of carbs and maybe some alcohol, you and all your colleagues would go home and sleep for two or three hours. You'd awake refreshed, alert, and much more capable of taking on the day's remaining tasks. You would arise safe in the knowledge that the two or three hours you spent in dreamland would have only been wasted fighting sleep at your desk, or—even worse—fighting sleep as you struggled through the pharmaceutical-grade sleep remedy known as the midafternoon meeting, which, in case you didn't see it coming, is what you are doing right now.

It's such a cruel joke, scheduling meetings right after lunch, when full consciousness is about as attainable as a winning lottery ticket. Especially meetings pertaining to expense report reimbursements and budgetary line item additions. *Double especially* when this information is being delivered by the company's head of accounting, a man with the most droning, hypnosis-inducing voice you have ever heard in your life. And the meeting just started five minutes ago. Here are some hacks to keep you awake.

Lazy Girl Hack: Keep Your Eyes Open

A classic approach to seeming awake during a meeting is to paint eyes onto your eyelids. This is a trick you'll need to do beforehand, so either do it at home or slip into the ladies' room. You might want to make the faux eyes a little bit bigger than your own natural eyes, so you'll seem almost ridiculously alert. You can even get the eyes tattooed permanently on your lids! Try to maintain as straight a posture as you can while slipping off into your siesta, so that you'll seem wide-eyed, attentive, and eager to learn. Try not to snore. You should also try not to drool, since an unblinking stare and nonstop drooling might give the accounting director the mistaken idea that you have a crush on him.

Okay, that's crazy talk, but you should really try to keep your eyes open. Even if you're struggling, let the struggle keep you awake.

You Know You're a Lazy Girl When . . .

Your most powerful moves at work are the power-naps you take in your car during your lunch break.

Lazy Girl Hack: Periodically Ask Questions

You probably will be jarred out of your REM sleep at a few points during this meeting anyway, so you should try to make use of your occasional wakefulness to ask a question or two. Jolting awake suddenly does draw attention to you, so when that happens, just ask a general question like, "How do we facilitate this?" or "What is the value proposition?" If just waking up makes you seem really startled when you ask these questions, all the better—you will seem very concerned, even urgently so. Asking questions or making comments during a meeting definitely makes it seem as though you are conscious and maybe even paying attention.

Lazy Girl Hack: Think about Getting Fired

One way to try to genuinely stay awake during a meeting is to imagine getting fired over it. Picture the boss calling you into her office, closing the door in that horrible telltale way, and saying those chilling words, “This just isn’t working out.” Then imagine having no money for the rent and having to live with your mom, who will leave classified ad clippings on your childhood bed, make you go with her to bridge night with her old-lady friends, and try to fix you up with her dentist, who has a hairy mole and smells like geriatric teeth. Imagine having to get a job dressing up as a giant slice of pizza and waving at people on the interstate. Imagine marrying the awful dentist in desperation and then never being able to feign sleep because you’ve had open eyes tattooed on your lids. Imagine all this, and if it doesn’t wake you up, I don’t know what will!

PROBLEM

You Hate Talking on the Phone, but Need to Suck It Up

Once upon a time, there used to be a thing called telephone customer service. In these olden days, many years ago, telephones were not used to reroute, confuse, frustrate, or musically torture callers. Customer service representatives did not play the hilarious game of wearing callers down with endless robotized prompts, dial-by-name directories, and menu options that were always being "recently changed." Back then, you didn't have to give a different name every time you answered and tell the customer the exact opposite of what you'd said the last time. You actually answered the phone when it rang (it actually rang!), and you just answered the question as best as you could. You didn't record the call for quality assurance purposes, or subject callers to long blocks of hold time while encouraging them to go online instead. Sometimes, you even *called people back*.

These days, as we all know, the only way to get that kind of personalized telephone service is to call a phone sex line. Even a torture fantasy with a telephone dominatrix is more merciful than trying to navigate the robo mind games of the typical customer service line. But since everything old eventually gets recycled as "retro," there will inevitably come the day when your boss longs for those golden days of great service. At this time you will have to actively *try* to help the other person on the line, even if only ironically. Here are some hacks for providing great customer service without feeling like you're the one being punished.

Lazy Girl Hack: Be Human

If you are an employee who wants to fake being helpful over the phone, you are in great luck. The bar for telephone helpfulness has never been lower. Telephone "customer service" is more of an ironic mockery of itself than anything else. People who call seeking help on the phone fully expect to be disappointed and messed with. So if you can actually sound human and helpful, you will blow their little minds. For starters, try not to sound like a robot. This will be difficult at first, since you've probably been trained to do the opposite, but after a while, it will start to feel almost natural. Go out of your way to be empathetic to the caller's problem, tell him about a time you had the same problem, and maybe make a joke or two. Most of all, don't actively try to subvert callers or be obviously unhelpful. You can even tell them your first and last names, and if you're allowed, your extension or direct number. Wow!

You Know You're a Lazy Girl When . . .

You tell the person you have a phone call with that you can only talk to him for fifteen minutes because you have a meeting that you need to get to. (Hint: There's no meeting.)

Lazy Girl Hack: Do Something for Them

Depending on your company and its particular objectives and rules, your hands may be tied as far as helping the customer. But if you can do a little bit to resolve the caller's issue, he might just start a religion in your name. If you're acting human and being kind, he's already eating out of your hand. So see if you can actually work on helping this fellow human out. Just imagine what it would be like for you if a customer service rep actually helped you. It would be amazing! That is how this person will feel if you give him what he asked for.

I would advise you to tread carefully with this "helping people" stuff—if you establish yourself as too much of an overachiever, the rest of your office might resent you. There's no need to be a "goody-goody." Or even "good." Just do the bare minimum—it will be way more than anyone has seen in years.

PROBLEM

Your Coworkers Have Exciting Weekend Plans, but You Plan to Catch Up on Netflix

Maybe you sit next to your office's resident socialite, who has something awesome going on every single weekend (and whose purse Chihuahua keeps shimmying into your snack drawer and eating all of your "I-live-at-the-office" treats). Or perhaps you still have to interact with that cute guy you went on a few awkward dates with before he never called you again. Or perhaps there's a not-so-cute guy who shows up at your cubicle each Thursday at noon to inquire about your weekend plans.

Whatever your motivation, you don't want to be the girl with nothing on the agenda this weekend but a rerun marathon, the alphabetizing of your Blu-ray collection, and the introduction of a tiny basketball hoop into your fish tank. Although these are all perfectly valid activities, they are dead giveaways that you "have a life" only in the literal sense that you have a pulse and are circulating blood. In fact, if someone were to check your pulse, insinuating that you might be undead, that would be a huge compliment. You *wish* you had the social life of a vampire!

Now, as if you weren't already giving your entire week to this job, it seems you're also required to maintain some sort of weekend "image control." You must conceal the fact that most of your weekends are about as exciting as a hand sanitizer convention. You know this because you've attended a hand sanitizer convention.

Lazy Girl Hack: Enlist a Friend's Help

One of the best strategies for broadcasting your oh-so-exciting weekend plans is to get a phone call from a friend discussing said plans. You have a few choices for how to play this one: You can either discuss your plans in a loud voice, so that everyone can hear all about them, or you can discuss them in a loud whisper, which is even better. The loud whisper will intrigue your audience, because it implies a juicy secret, but it's so flipping loud everyone will be able to hear it anyway. So, it's both attention-grabbing and exhibitionistic, while also seeming "discreet." During your conversation, be sure to say lots of things that imply exciting scandal, like, "OMG! Please tell me he is *not* going show his face there! Are you kidding? Does he know she's coming too? Oh, this is going to be *awesome*!"

You can also drop little clues that suggest that you're incredibly popular, such as "Well, hmm, maybe I will stop by that party for a while, and then meet up with you guys at the club later."

The phone call can either be a real, interactive call with a friend (or your mom, if you're really desperate) who agrees to contact you at a strategic time, or you can do a faux cell phone exchange with no one on the other end. Choose your words carefully—note that women who like to go out to wild parties are fond of calling each other "babe" and "sweetie." So say things like, "Okay, babe, meet you at the club at ten!" Your mom will love your new term of endearment for her.

Lazy Girl Hack: Enlist the Help of Photoshop and Social Media

You can also broadcast your awesome weekend after the fact through Photoshopped pics posted on Facebook. Put you and your girlfriends in all sorts of crazy scenarios—doing shots off some guy's abs, doing shots off a rhinoceros's horn, doing shots off a newborn baby's head (careful of the soft spot!). This strategy is sort of situation-specific, though—you can't stop the nerdy guy in IT from asking you out today by showing him a photo from the future. But you can always tell him you're going out with your friends, and then he'll see the proof that you did it. He'll also see that you are a wild and crazy creature, and that he clearly has no shot.

PROBLEM

You Need to Ditch a Meeting, but Don't Know What to Say

Your week has been nothing but back-to-back meetings—meetings about current work projects, meetings about when to have another meeting, meetings about whether maybe your company has too many meetings (the answer: no way!). The hilarious part—if it didn't also make you want to cry—is that rather than sitting in a meeting talking about these projects, you could be at your desk actually *working* on them. Instead, you've been doodling what you hope will someday be artistic masterpieces that will enable you to quit your job.

In fact, there's a meeting scheduled for this afternoon, in which you are supposed to report to the higher-ups about how one of your projects is coming along. The truth is, it's *not* coming along, because almost every waking hour of your recent history has been sucked up into meetings. You would think they would somehow understand this, but they don't. You're beginning to suspect that these meeting freaks have discovered a traversable wormhole through which they are able to go back in time. It's totally unfair that they haven't shared this with you.

Regardless, your meeting is on the books for 2:00 p.m., and you're just not ready. You need to bust out of this place for the day—but you have to fake it convincingly. Enter the following lazy girl hacks!

Lazy Girl Hack: Use an App!

Yes, of course there are apps for getting out of meetings—are you really surprised? Some of them allow you to schedule an "emergency text" to come in at a certain time. You can just read the text and say, "Oops! It seems my hot water heater exploded and my apartment is flooded. I have to go take care of that." Another service interrupts you with an urgent phone call, which will provide a recorded "repeat after me" voice telling you exactly which words to utter. You'll be fed lines like, "Oh my God. Where are you right now?" and, "Okay, calm down. I'll be right there." It's better than having to come up with your own impromptu dialogue in front of your boss and colleagues. Many of these services are cheap or free, so go for it—but use it sparingly, or they *will* catch on to you.

Lazy Girl Hack: Put Your Pet to Work

All you really need to do to get out of work early is pretend to have a pet emergency. Something's come up and you really have to take Mittens in to the vet office. If that doesn't tear at the heartstrings of your boss, you should definitely consider changing jobs. Who doesn't care about an animal's life? No one you want to work with, that's for damn sure!

PROBLEM

You Have to Work with a Coworker, but Have No Idea Who She Is

Maybe you're at the company picnic and have been randomly paired up for the egg toss competition with someone who has never said "boo" to you—or worse, someone who *has* said "boo" to you. Or maybe you've been sent on a business trip to Dubai with a guy you don't know from Adam (at least they didn't send Adam—that guy's a real creep). Or maybe an important client asks you if you know his favorite sales associate, let's call her Person-You-Have-Never-Interacted-with-Except-the-Time-You-Burned-Popcorn-in-the Lunchroom-and-You-Smiled-Sheepishly-at-Her-As-You-Slunk-Away-in-a-Trail-of-Smoke. Actually, that's kind of long. Let's call her Lisa.

The reality is that most offices keep people as compartmentalized in their little cubicles as zoo animals in cages. We rarely move outside our own little enclosures to interact with those exotic species in other departments.

To the outside world, though, we're supposed to seem united, a team, aware of one another's existence. So when you get thrown into an unexpected collaboration with an unfamiliar coworker, you need to act like you're on the same team. Ideally, the other person will recognize the need for this fakery and play along. If not, you may have to appoint yourself imaginary team captain and call the plays until your teammate picks up on your strategy and starts executing the fakes like an old pro. If you do it right, the two of you will hit this thing right out of the park—unless we're talking about the egg toss at the picnic. In that case, please be gentle and do not hit the egg at all.

Lazy Girl Hack: Focus on Your Common Goal

If you were playing a game of soccer, you wouldn't need to know your teammate well to pass the ball for a game-winning goal, would you? No. You would just know what your roles were on the team and relate to each other that way. If you were the pitcher and your coworker was the catcher, you wouldn't need to be BFFs to understand her elaborate hand signals and weird finger wiggling, right? Hardly. If you were on the same professional wrestling team, you wouldn't have to be pals with your partner, Buff Bagwell, to let him break a chair on your head as a trick on your opponents, the Wolfpac, would you? Yes, a wooden chair. Yes, directly onto your face—what else are chairs for?

Anyway, the point of this is that you and your colleague already have a lot in common: namely, a shared mission. If you focus on your common goal, whether it's acing a presentation or not getting chair splinters in your eyes, you will bond surprisingly quickly.

Lazy Girl Hack: Drop Names, but Don't Drop the Ball

So, suppose you have to fake knowing a coworker without the advantage of that person being there to play along. For example, let's say you have an important new client, Alistair Shmoe, and you're meeting with him for the first time. He says, "You work at X Company, so you *must* know Blah Blah." Unfortunately, you have never met Blah Blah and know next to nothing about him.

But you don't want to stare blankly at your new client, or ask him who the hell Blah Blah is. Even worse, you don't want to take a wild guess at some tidbit of information to prove you know the man. You should simply say something vague but positive about Blah Blah. You can say something like, "Blah Blah does good work. I haven't worked closely with him, but I've heard good things." Perfect. You seem in the know, but not like a know-it-all. Go team!

PROBLEM

You Don't Know the Answer to Your Client's Question, but Your Boss Is Watching

It's been a long day, and just as you're about to pack up and go home, you get a call from an important client. She's asking if your company would be able to supply her with 150 units of Product X and 200 units of Product Y by close of business on Friday. (They're all good on Zs, apparently. So are you, as evidenced by the contents of the cartoon thought bubble over your head.)

You are an ambitious, relatively new associate at your company, and you would love to dazzle this woman by promising her more Xs and Ys than a chromosomal hermaphrodite. However, you have no idea how long it would take your company to produce 150 of Product X, and you're not even sure what product Y is. Now what?

Well, of course, the last thing you want to sound like is exactly what you are: a new person who isn't really sure what she's doing yet. There's something off-putting about customer service that whittles down to a fancy equivalent of "duh."

But how do you fake knowing what you don't know without the thing you don't know coming back to bite you in the butt—especially when your boss's office is right around the corner from your desk and you know she can hear every word you say?

Lazy Girl Hack: Underpromise, Overdeliver

The whole underpromise/overdeliver trick is a little mind game that has worked well in business for many years. Nobody really minds that you've fibbed a bit in your underpromise, because your overdelivery is effing awesome.

It's sort of like an encore at a concert by your favorite band—the band's sort of like, "Bye, now! That was totally our last song, we swear! We are *definitely* not coming back, not even if you clap a whole lot!" When the band does come back onstage to play one last rousing song, you don't think, "What liars!" You think, "They surpassed my every expectation!" That's the crux of the old underpromise/overdeliver strategy.

So how this would work is you tell your client, "Nope, we definitely do not have any Xs or Ys, that's for sure. Sorry, lady, but there are no ifs, ands, or buts about our Xs and Ys." Then go find out if there really are any Xs or Ys, and if there are enough to meet her request, make it seem like you moved mountains to get them for her. The only potential problem here is if she has already moved on to another vendor for her Xs and Ys. Then your overdelivery would be more like overkill. And when it comes to kill, people usually prefer underkill or just the right amount of kill.

Lazy Girl Hack: Admit You Don't Know

According to Janine Popick, writing for www.inc.com, it's not always the best idea to pretend you know the answer when you don't. There's a name for that type of person—a know-it-all.

As much as a client might huff and puff about your admitting that you don't know, they will ultimately appreciate the fact that you value their time enough to be honest. Imagine if you promised them all the Xs and Ys they could handle, and then later had to tell them it turns out your company doesn't even make Xs or Ys?

You Know You're a Lazy Girl When . . .
You only restart your computer when your programs start to crash.

Of course, you can dress this up a bit—you don't have to come right out and say, "Um, I have absolutely no clue." Instead, maybe say something like, "Listen, I just want to check and make sure we have the resources to help you with this. I will get right back to you." Then you can call them back or email them with the answer. Even if they don't love your answer this time, they will remember you as a straight shooter who takes time to do the research before you speak. It's simple professionalism. Look, people dislike know-it-alls even in kindergarten—why should that change now?

PROBLEM

Your Boss References Something, but You Don't Know What He Means

So, you started a new job in your chosen field, the vocation you studied extensively over the course of your four years in college. You think you know what the job requires of you, and since you were hired, you can only assume your boss feels the same. Then, during the first week of your employment, your boss and various higher-ups said many terrible and confusing things to you. Things like:

"We need to drill down to the ROI and develop a turnkey solution."

"We need a silver bullet from those thought leaders. I don't want to shoot the puppy on this one."

"Ping me about the mature onboarding. We need to use best practice methodology to incentivize our supply chain."

You *thought* you understood this job; for that matter, you *thought* you understood the English language. But after hearing your boss spout this gibberish, you're pretty sure your job is to translate from the native language of planet Uranus.

Corporations like to come up with their own encoded language—which to an outsider sounds terribly confusing—to trick the world into thinking they are doing something very technical and difficult. In reality, they're probably watching YouTube videos of foxes jumping on trampolines. Regardless, though, you need to understand your boss—and he can't, or won't, speak normally.

Lazy Girl Hack: Pick Up on Context Clues

Eventually, you will begin to decipher this language just by observing the meaning of the words in context. For example, if someone is supposed to get "pinged" and they remain uninjured by the end of the day, then it didn't involve being shot with a BB gun, as you originally thought. If someone who was given a "golden parachute" never comes back to the office again, it didn't mean they were destined to "rise to the top," like you'd assumed. And all that worry you put yourself through after your boss said your idea was "hand grenade close" was completely unnecessary. Turns out that didn't mean it was a total bomb, or, in the language of *Jersey Shore*, an unattractive girl. It was actually a compliment!

Other terms can be decoded by how they sound. "Smirting," for example, is a hybrid of smoking and flirting, and, accordingly, means flirting with coworkers during a smoke break. "Sympvertising" is advertising aimed at consumers' sympathy. So just spend some time watching and listening, and eventually you'll understand the meanings through cause and effect. Hopefully, you'll figure it out before you get the golden parachute!

Lazy Girl Hack: Consult a Glossary

You'll be relieved to know that many people are, like you, utterly dumbfounded by many of the references made in the workplace. As a result, there are many glossaries of corporate jargon and office-speak. Some of them are books and some are websites, but all of them attempt to clarify and demystify this weird nonlanguage used in offices. For example, you'll find out what an "ear job" is, or a "brain dump," or "management porn" (thank God this does not involve your boss in an X-rated film). These resources are not only useful in cracking the code a little bit faster, but they're tremendously amusing. You definitely will want to drill down into this brain dump!

Once you do learn and master corporate jargon, the next step is to not use it. It's one thing to understand it—that will help you to get by and ping effectively. But most of the time corporate speak not only doesn't make a person sound smarter, it also makes them less likable to others. So you should set yourself apart from your colleagues, and be the person who speaks clear English. Everyone will want you to give them an ear job!

PROBLEM

You're Dragged Into Drama at the Office, but Don't Want to Overreact

You've probably had a job where some smarty-pants manager has told you that you'll need to "check your ego at the door," "check your baggage at the door," or "check your crazy obsession with the water cooler delivery guy at the door." If only! Imagine what an incredible baggage check system that would be! At the end of the day, when you see your wacko emotional issues going around the carousel, you could just leave them there.

In reality, as much as we professional people try to pretend otherwise, we all show up for work with a full set of working emotions. We can try to curb them (at least the negative ones) all we want, but they still exist.

In many ways, your most basic emotions—anger, fear, sadness, jealousy—haven't evolved much from the way they were when you were five years old. Thus, when these emotions are allowed to rule, you could potentially act like a five-year-old throwing a fit. Not good for your chances for a promotion.

So when your boss is getting on your case about something totally unfair—your coworker gets a promotion you know you deserved, or your clients are tormenting you with last-minute demands in the face of a deadline—how do you keep that explosive five-year-old at bay? Believe it or not, an ice cream cone is only part of the answer. Here's the rest.

Lazy Girl Hack: Buy Time and Breathe

Take a page from your mom's book and count to ten and take a breath. Of course, you should *not* threaten to flog colleagues at the end of ten seconds, especially if it's your boss. Instead, this should be a private thing, wherein you retreat inside to a happy place and practice yogic breathing while not saying the horrible, career-destroying thing you want to say. Will it look weird, you standing there and taking measured breaths after your coworker waits for you to reply to the verbal dump he just unloaded on you? Maybe—but it's much better to be known as "That Weird Woman Who Doesn't Say Anything for Ten Full One-Mississippi Seconds" than "That Woman Who Told the Boss That He Clearly Has a Napoleon Complex of the Penis," otherwise known as "That Woman Who No Longer Works Here."

An even better way to buy time is to simply suck up your emotions, walk away, and continue the conversation over email. Once you have retreated to the safe haven of the Internet, you can put your meltdown on ice and craft a composed, rational, and emotionally neutral version of your thoughts on the matter. In other words, say the exact opposite of what you feel. If, in reviewing the email, you notice a sentence that speaks to your gut instincts, tweak it right away. After all, that's the beauty of the Internet: there is never any need for a kneejerk reaction, unless your knee has a ridiculously delayed jerk mechanism. If so, don't worry—there are probably drugs for that.

Lazy Girl Hack: Find a Venting Buddy

Chances are, there is at least one person at your office who is discreet, trustworthy, and starved for gossip. If you have someone in your office that you trust, head to her desk to vent to about your stress, anger, disappointment, and jealousy. You don't want to wallow or talk her ear off, but maybe a little lunchtime venting session will help you blow off some of that steam. Possibly, your friend will offer some perspective or commiseration—perhaps something along the lines of, "Oh, I've had the exact same problem with X."

Keep in mind, too, that although venting is best known for its fulfilling emotional purge, it can also lead to a useful exchange of ideas, and even some great fakes. Your friend might be well versed in corporate speak and provide you with the words you need (e.g., "I've had a robust pre-think with the team, and we're vectoring toward going live with this ASAP") to get X off your back until you actually figure this mess out.

Lazy Girl Hack: Remember, Bad Days End

It's true that you can't leave your emotions at the door of your office when you arrive at work in the morning, and likewise, you can't leave them at the office when you go home. But try to remember that a bad day is just that—a bad day. You can go home, take a hot bath, eat some fudge walnut brownies, drink some wine, and go to bed. Maybe after a night's sleep, a small pity soiree, and some time away, you'll have a better perspective on how to handle the issue, or at least be able to suck up your pride and lie about your feelings for the greater good. And you'll be so happy you got through the day without kicking your boss right in the source of his troublesome testosterone! You deserve another glass of wine just for that!

PROBLEM

Your Manager Wants You to Step Up, but You're Clueless

Whoever came up with the expression "There's no such thing as a stupid question" has clearly never met your boss. He's one of those guys who rattles off, in one impatient sentence, a request for you to split the atom by the end of the day, then concludes with, "You can handle that, right?" In case you didn't know, there's only one acceptable answer to that question, and it isn't "I want my mommy."

Of course, Mr. Vague is also notoriously annoyed by follow-up questions, even ones that are perfectly reasonable. Now, he's paid you the "compliment" of assigning you a very important, almost entirely incomprehensible project. He just stopped at your desk, cleared his throat, and uttered such a rapid-fire, nonsensical mash-up of corporate jargon and SAT vocabulary words that you're not even sure what your name is anymore. Well, whatever your name is, Boss Crazyhead is trusting you with something you don't even think you can pronounce. Don't worry, lazy girl. You'll make it through this too.

Lazy Girl Hack: Ask for a Sample or Template

Since it seems that much of your boss's leadership technique relies upon the mind-reading capabilities of his underlings, and you, unfortunately, don't possess those powers, read up on how other coworkers tackled the project. If this assignment involves a written report or other document, ask your boss if you can study some of the materials from previous projects of this nature—particularly ones that were done well. Just say that you want to study the materials so you can understand what sets a successful effort apart. This will make you seem ambitious and thorough, without revealing you don't know what the hell you are doing. Hopefully, if you can get your mitts on some previous samples of this type of work, they will give you clues about how it should be done. It'll be like solving a murder mystery, except you'll actually be preventing a murder—the murder of your career. Or your boss.

Lazy Girl Hack: Talk to Someone Who's Been There

Hopefully, the project you've been assigned is something that someone else in your office has handled before (who *hasn't* split an atom at some point?). If this is the case, choose someone who seems understanding and empathetic, maybe treat her to lunch, and ask her for some pointers. Again, you don't need to volunteer the information that you're absolutely clueless, although if you're lucky, she might tell you that she once felt the same way. Make sure to be cautious about saying anything negative about the boss, though. Probably everyone knows he's a freak, but you don't want to be the person who says it out loud.

The good news is you've found someone who is willing to share his or her wisdom with you. Learn everything you can from this person, and before you know it, you will genuinely know what you're doing!

PROBLEM

You Have to Give a Presentation, but Have Major Imposter Syndrome

You're fairly new at your job, and you've been working like a dog. Fortunately, all this effort has paid off! Your boss is so impressed with your diligence and hard work that she wants *you* to give an important presentation for your department to the company's entire board of directors.

Ack! Reward? You might prefer a *reward* that involves being placed on a wooden rack and being stretched in separate directions until you can hear your joints forcibly dislocating. Public speaking, unfortunately, is just not your thing and you're not really sure that you even deserve to be the one who spearheads the presentation.

Like it or not, though, this seems to be your big chance to get on the radar of the company bigwigs. You've been working all this time to make a name for yourself. You just don't want that name to be "Awkward McFreakout."

Lazy Girl Hack: Prepare Yourself!

As everyone knows, the best way to overcome your nerves and look confident during a presentation is to be prepared. If you know your material well and have enthusiasm for it, that feeling will resonate. Practice your speech in front of a small group of friends, or a mirror. Don't break the mirror—it's much better to break your leg. A fracture of your femur means your speech will turn out well, but a breakage of a $7.50 mirror from Kmart spells disaster. Plus, if you are lucky enough to break your leg, everyone will be so focused on your cast that they won't care about your presentation.

Lazy Girl Hack: Use Visual Aids

If you are a self-conscious individual (this means *you*, lazy girl), the last thing you are going to want is to have everyone staring at you during the entire presentation. If you feel the fiery laser heat of thirty-five high-ranking pairs of eyes on you as you speak, you're likely to break under the pressure (and I don't mean your other leg, either—you should be so lucky).

A great way to divert the attention from you and put it back on the content is the use of visual media. You can use a PowerPoint presentation, charts or graphs, illustrations, or even a video if applicable. Not only will this take the heat off you, it will help keep your audience awake. The human attention span is pretty limited, so if you can give them some new, colorful stuff to look at, they'll be as mesmerized as a baby staring at those multicolored plastic keys. Remember, if you are using PowerPoint slides with information on them, don't simply read that same information aloud; it's redundant. Instead, elaborate a little bit on what the slide is showing.

Lazy Girl Hack: Focus on the Message

Another useful strategy in keeping your composure during a presentation is to remind yourself that this isn't about you. You are simply the conduit, the instrument through which this important information is being conveyed. This is something these folks need to know about, and you need to tell them. If the building were on fire and you went to tell your coworkers that smoke and flames were ravaging the cafeteria, you wouldn't think, "OMG, do I look fat in this burning skirt? Did I stutter over the words 'smoke inhalation'?" Well, maybe you would. But your first concern would be to communicate the essential facts: Fire. Building. Here.

Look, the truth is, this is about you. But that's something for you to revel in later, after you've totally nailed it. For now, just focus on the message, and make sure you get the essentials out there. So, are you out of intact leg bones at this point? Then break an arm!

INDEX

ABOUT THE AUTHOR

Jennifer Byrne writes humorous essays, satire, and journalistic pieces. Her writing has been published online in *The New Yorker*, *Huffington Post*, *The Rumpus*, *The Hairpin*, *The Second City Network*, *National Lampoon*, and more.